HELLO MEXICO!

HELLO MEXICO!

HOW AMERICANS CAN GET ALONG
AND ENJOY LIVING IN MEXICO

by
Lorrain Giddings

toExcel
San Jose New York Lincoln Shanghai

Hello Mexico!
How Americans can get along and enjoy living in Mexico

This edition published by toExcel Press,
an imprint of iUniverse.com, Inc.

For information address:
iUniverse.com, Inc.
620 North 48th Street
Suite 201
Lincoln, NE 68504-3467
www.iuniverse.com

ISBN: 1-58348-766-2

Acknowledgments

I'm indebted to many people, family and friends. They read my manuscript and gave me corrections and suggestions. I believe I made all the corrections, and I followed many of the suggestions. Still, the final responsibility for the book is mine alone.

CONTENTS

1
WHY THIS BOOK

Here is why I wrote this book and why you might want to read it.

There is a major change afoot in the three countries of North America. The North American Free Trade Agreement, NAFTA, was signed a few years ago. This one was not forced by anyone on anyone else, like most territorial treaties with Mexico years ago. This one is just a reflection of realities of the modern world, and Mexico wants and needs to be a functional part of the modern world.

Mexico has always needed a closer economic alliance with the US. Mexico still produces people with such efficiency that many of them emigrate to the US. At the same time, the US has needed laborers, and hasn't been producing them. The answer has been to automate more and more, with a nearly-hidden dependence on illegal migrant labor, but there are limits to all things. The more reasonable solution has been for more cooperation, but for many reasons, this has never worked. At last, Mexico has taken that major step that should allow it to grow economically in ways that it needs, and it seems to be working.

It's simply a new world. Mexico has a lot of adapting to do. The US has to adapt, too, but that won't be so hard. The big problem for the US is to understand something more about Mexico. The rules that govern Mexico are not really written rules, and they aren't the kind Americans are accustomed to thinking about. But if Americans don't learn how things work in Mexico, they will get hurt.

This book is an irreverent introduction to these rules, for Americans. I intend to tell you the things you won't find in Mexican travel books. Those books tell you the superficial things about visiting Mexico: the feast days, the hotels you can use, where to rent cars, how to get to different places, the handicrafts you can buy, all those things. I'll tell you what life is really like in this lovely country, but without the varnish of a travel folder. It's the human story, not the tourist story.

Who am I to write this? I'm an American, a permanent resident of Mexico. I've been here for two decades. I enjoy living here, and I want to continue. I'm a Gringo, rather older now than I'd like, with a Mexican wife and teenage Mexican-American children. I've learned a bit from living here, and I remember how it was when I came.

You should find this book useful. Let me give you an example, one that won't leave the back of my mind. I remember when I was young enough to just want to travel and understand other parts of the world. It was obvious that American suburbia was not the whole picture, but I hadn't seen anything else at that age. So with some friends I went driving to Mexico. That opened a new world for me.

That trip wasn't very important, but I will tell you about the last time I drove from the US back to Mexico, many years later. I was driving along, my family in the car, when just ahead of us there was one of those terrible accidents that used to be so common in Mexico. Two people in the little car died, the third will never be whole again, and the truck that ended up on top of them, well, that driver will never forget the incident.

What got my attention, and should get yours, is that the tourists were young Americans, just like I was when I first went to Mexico. They were riding along one minute, and the next they were in great pain or dead, and all because they did not know the rules.

What rules? It's just that traffic is different in Mexico. Not the official rules in the books you can buy; those rules are, by and large, the same. I mean the rules people actually live and drive by. Those young people didn't know the *real* rules of the road in Mexico, and for that innocent ignorance they paid a terrible price.

You need to know all the real rules of life in Mexico. If I'm successful, this will be a practical book for you. It will awaken you to understand Mexicans and Mexico better. And if it does really well, it could even save your life.

And if it's really successful, it may even make you want to live here permanently. But don't. That's too much success. I want to live in Mexico with Mexicans. I don't want this to become another US. Mexico is just fine as Mexico.

What We Call Each Other

Here I'm going to use the word, *American*, to refer to citizens of the United States of America, *Mexican* to refer to citizens of Mexico, and *Canadian* to refer to citizens of Canada.

What's wrong with that? Well, with *Canadian* there's no problem. And with *Mexican* there's very little problem.

But Mexicans (and not just a few other groups) don't like the term, *American*. Since *America* means all of North, Central and South America, they don't like people from the US preempting the term. I don't much like it either, since between northern Canada and Southern Argentina and Chile, we are certainly all Americans.

But there is no other good term. Mexicans like to call Americans *North Americans*, but outside of Mexico, that obviously won't do. Mexicans and Canadians are also North Americans: they live in North America, and they are part of the *North American Free Trade Agreement*. And it's obviously unreasonable to call them *North-Americans-Who-Aren't-Canadians-or-Mexicans* or the *other North Americans*.

In some countries, Americans are called *United Statesians* (*estadounidenses* in Spanish). But that's not so good either. Actually, the formal name of Mexico is the *United Mexican States (Estados Unidos Mexicanos)*, so Mexicans are also United Statesians.

So let's let the Americans decide what to call themselves in English, and let's let everybody else call them what they choose. Here I choose to call them *Americans*.

Actually, the only country with *America* in the formal name is the United States of America, and for that, the Americans justify calling themselves Americans when they bother to do any justifying. *America* is two continents, but it's also a country.

Still, even I have a problem with using *America* to refer to the country, United States of America. So I'll use *US* to refer to that country, even though I recognize the ambiguity. After all, I've never seen *US* used to refer to Mexico, even though it's also appropriate.

Occasionally I'll talk about *Gringos* and *Gringoland*. We *Gringos* are all those people from the US culture. With some people, it means only *palefaces*, and with others it means everybody from European or Canadian or American cultures, but I'll refer only to the US, and to people of all shades and colors. And just like *Disneyland* is the land of the Disney spectacles, *Gringoland* is the home of the Gringos. (I, of course, am a *Gringo*, though I don't live in *Gringoland*.)

So in this book, *Canadians* are Canadians, *Mexicans* are Mexicans, and *Americans* are Americans. *Canada* is Canada, *Mexico* is the country of Mexico, and *US* is the United States of America. Also, Mexico City is *Mexico City* (whereas Mexicans tend to just call the city *Mexico*). *Gringoland* is where all the *Gringos* live. Once you put this book down, go back to calling everybody what you will (within limits, please).

How This Book is Arranged

I do need to tell you how this book is arranged. I'm going to start with the three things that get everybody's attention: the status of families, corruption, and money. These serve as something of a background to everything else, things that simply can never, and should never be forgotten.

Then I talk about one of the most joyful of things in Mexico, the food, and I'll try to give you rules to help you enjoy eating without paying the price that many foreigners pay. Closely related to food are medicine and health, my next subjects.

Then I'll talk about what is the most foreign and bothersome to Americans: the police. This is the chapter that's hardest to write, and that I most didn't want to write, but it's very important you understand this problem. Closely related to this is the general status of politics in Mexico, which is also quite different than most people in the US are accustomed to.

Even if you skip all of the above, read the chapters on driving in Mexico. They can, and should, save your life if you're thinking of even driving a little. Learn the *real* rules of driving. Driving can be a pleasant experience, or it can lead to an unimaginable nightmare. It's not necessary to drive at all in Mexico, but if you're thinking of driving even a little, pay a lot of attention to these chapters, *please*!!!

From here on out I talk about things that I think might be interesting to you. Believe it or not, I suggest you pay attention to the Mexican style of catch-as-catch-can wrestling, mostly known in the US as "professional wrestling," which, of course, is not wrestling at all. Then I urge you not be afraid of Spanish as a language. Compared to most others, it's not very hard to learn, and I think you'll enjoy it.

For those of you who are really flexible, I suggest you just give in and accept the country as it is. This is the way you'll best understand it. That doesn't mean you'll stop being a Gringo, but it does give you a parallel way of living that you can slip into very comfortably when you want. That's what I try to do, and it makes things much nicer.

Finally I talk about some other things that may be of interest. There's the question of servants if you choose to move here (I tell you that you should have servants, for many reasons). Then there are some off-beat things you can do to enjoy and better understand Mexico. One is simply to explore markets, and the other is to explore the countryside in a distinctly non-Gringo way.

Opinions!

I must say very explicitly that I am only giving opinions and personal interpretations in this book. I'm telling you what I believe I see, and I'm giving you my opinions on what those things mean. I am not pretending to give you the truth about anything. I'm not even sure there is such a thing as truth in most of these cases.

If my opinions and interpretations here are useful to you, and if they help you avoid misunderstandings, then I'll be happy and your money will have been well spent.

I'm full of good advice and good suggestions. But I definitely don't give legal advice, nor do I give advice that is binding in any way. All I'm doing is suggesting things I think will help you enjoy and understand this country, and do it in a safe way.

I'm especially interested in having you enjoy your visit here, so I only suggest what looks safest to me. Still, you must understand that you, yourself, take responsibility for anything you do.

2

THE FAMILY GAME

I have always prided myself on having a good American family. We all like each other, and we all know each other. I'm even still in contact with one of my first cousins. But compared to my wife's family, that's nothing at all. "Family" is the first broad theme that you should understand.

Family is big in Mexico. It's a background to most activities, personal and business. You do need to understand the concept because it affects almost everything.

The Concept of Family is Different

As for me, I think of my family as my parents, my wife and kids, my brothers and sisters; I could stretch things and include my nieces and nephews, and if there were any, grandparents and grandchildren would certainly be included. I know who my aunts and uncles and my first cousins were. And since *family* was big (for the US) in my family, I even once knew a few cousins of my parents.

I suppose at the moment I could identify twenty or thirty living family members, but that's because we're a relatively strong family. Most people I know couldn't give the names of more than ten or so, depending on how many brothers and sisters they had.

My wife, on the other hand, is Mexican. She can recite the names and relationship of some 600 or 800 family members. When we married, in Mexico City, she explained that we would have just a small family affair. Small for Mexico, maybe, but some 500 people showed up, all relatives, and most relatives couldn't come for one reason or another!

I'm even very interested in my family: I know my genealogy.

On the other hand, my wife really knows her *family*.

What does all this mean? It means that family life is fundamentally different. Given some reasonable precautions, life is better in Mexico. Family values do exist. It's certainly easier to raise kids in Mexico.

But it also means that the rules are not what you expect. As usual, you need to understand.

The Safety Net

Life is harder in Mexico. Jobs are not that easy to find, and things tend to work slowly. You don't just go out and get a job. Unless it's a rather menial job, you apply, in time you are evaluated, and a few months later, you learn whether you have a job or not. It depends on the job, of course, but normally you do not just apply and start work tomorrow or next week.

Assume that you as a young person decide to become a professional person of some kind. You go to college, and finish your course work, usually in five years. But you don't just get your degree. You have to apply for papers as an *egresado* (finished all course work), which requires red tape and wading through an ill-tempered college bureaucracy that has not the slightest interest in your getting your certificate.

But then you have to do some research, or whatever, that allows you to write an undergraduate thesis. Your professors are responsible for helping you, for sponsoring you, for reviewing your manuscript, and for examining you on your professional exam. But your professors receive no money nor recognition for doing this, and they are busy earning a living in addition to teaching college. So you take a year or two in the process, during which, unless you are extremely lucky, you can't hold down a job.

Or, you might lose your job, and it could take you months to get another. Or, sickness or an accident might make you unemployable for a while. Or, you may go to school in another town, but you don't have money for support there. Or, your parents might die in an accident. Or you and your wife might die, leaving kids.

These are all things that happen, that make you use the *family rescue net*. If you are an ordinary Mexican, and these things happen, your relatives will take care of you.

It happened to me. I lost my job. I was unemployed for four months. Although I didn't need to use the net, and I was not an ordinary Mexican, it was there. I was told many times that we (all of us) could move in with them. Who were they? Brothers-and sisters-in-law, cousins, and others. Who were we? A family of five. The word got around that we were unemployed, and the word got to this Gringo, who might not expect nor understand such things, that there was help available at any time.

And you know, there were even people who weren't even family, but who felt we had treated them like family that made the offer!

That was great!

The Other Side

That's how family looks to me, and to almost everybody else. It's a supportive organization. Mexicans learn how it works from the earliest conscious moment. They have parties with their cousins even before they can walk or talk with competence. It's family, family, family.

Now let's look at the other side. The family reflex doesn't just go away when a person grows up. It just grows a bit more informed. That is to say, a kid can only receive from the family. But when that kid grows to productive years, he will have a reflex to strengthen the family. What was once a passive acceptance can convert to an active passion.

In practice, what does this mean? Wherever a person is, family enters. Who do you buy from? Who gets the concession? Should that person be given a license for a business? Who can sell to the government? Who won the bidding?

Curiously, even when there's no legitimate personal family interest, family can still enter. If you look at the persons hired for services by an official of some organization, you may find that there is a family relationship with a friend or employee of that same official. It's not just that money is involved. People simply feel more comfortable if there's some kind of family tie involved!

As a Foreigner

Here, as a foreigner, you may have an inherent disadvantage compared to any Mexican because you aren't immersed in a Mexican family. You may feel this is a form of corruption, and by American standards, of course, it is. A Mexican, pressed, will admit that this is corruption in fact, but it's the normal way of doing business in Mexico.

If you're a Mexican, your reflex is always family. If you don't favor your family, it requires a deliberate effort, because your reflex is to look for the advantage for your family.

3
CORRUPTION IN THE
SCHEME OF THINGS

Corruption is a nasty word, but we have to understand something about it. Mexicans hate corruption as much as Americans, and they are doing just what the Americans did many years ago: insisting that it disappear. And it is disappearing, but slower than we'd like. Still, it's part of the current scene, and you need to know.

I do have to talk about "corruption." It's not an easy thing to talk about, because we have an automatic reflex against corruption. But it's something that's always with us, in Mexico or in the US, and we have to come to grips with it.

You need to think about the historical background of corruption in Mexico. If you ask a person that's say, 50 years old, he'll be just as opposed to corruption as you. He'll be scandalized by all sorts of things that are happening in politics and on the street. But if you ask him about some of the most admired of past political figures, he won't be as drastic.

Everybody recognizes that many of the previous presidents made personal fortunes while they were in office or as a result of being in office. I won't name names, but I'm not referring the last several presidents, who've coincided with financial problems, inflation, devaluations, and the like. I'm talking about the ones that worked at industrializing the country, that built the infrastructure of the great cities, and that exercised moral leadership of their communities in many ways. They managed the financial affairs of the nation with responsibility. They did not cause inflation, or devaluations. They created jobs for enough people that unemployment wasn't a serious problem. They are revered figures, even though most of them, maybe all, visibly increased their wealth while in office.

On the other hand, the more recent political leadership appears to have contributed little or nothing the country needs. They did personally get wealthier, there are evidently fewer jobs compared to the number of people needing work, and they certainly didn't manage the financial affairs of the nation with responsibility. They appear to have done very well for themselves at the cost of the rest of the country.

Coming from the American culture, I have severe problems with these ideas. If I knew that any otherwise revered American president got rich as a result of being president, I would certainly not consider him a worthy figure. But this is not my culture nor my country. It's not for me to judge the Mexican way of politics. As a matter of fact, it almost seems a feudal or a monarchical way of looking at things: the king and his barons are above scrutiny.

The upshot is that Mexicans are growing more like Americans in their approach to the corruption of their officials: more and more they are coming to a consensus that **almost** all corruption is bad and must cease.

So now, let's look at some specifics.

Corruption at the Highest Levels

The top levels of corruption are among the hardest to eliminate. Once the precedent has been set, the political descendants think they know the rules, and they proceed to act in the old molds. They may be the children of the elders, or they may simply be the newer politicians, entering the field mostly because of the opportunity to get rich.

Corruption at these levels is a constant theme in Mexican newspapers, and a constant theme in the speeches of political leaders and even in ordinary conversations. That is to say, it is a constant worry for Mexicans.

We are probably seeing the end of free plundering at the highest levels, simply because the country will no longer put up with it. It may have been relatively "appropriate" when Mexico was a truly undeveloped country, and it certainly it's rampant in most very poor countries. But it's certainly not appropriate for a modern Mexico.

But now it's hard to get away with major theft. Former governors and high officials are now in jail for complicity in theft of public funds. It's hard, but measures are being taken against theft at high levels. Given the long tradition of public theft by public "servants," the public is wary. But progress is evident.

Middle Levels

It used to be fairly easy to steal in all the middle levels of government, and major and minor family fortunes were made this way, by fake purchases, falsely billed purchases and contracts, and the like. The last several presidencies have instituted rigid measures to prevent this kind of theft, including a required reporting of personal wealth of all government employees above a quite low level. Unexplained enrichment is a serious crime.

There is certainly much less apparent theft in these levels. Still, most people feel it is still fairly strong. It's hard to know, but it's certainly less frequent than before.

But at the Bottom Levels

But the bottom levels are another problem. There are so many different types of activities involved that it is hard to control them all. And here we need to be honest: here, low wages play an important part. Even if a person can get a job, normally it's not easy to live on the wage that he earns.

In many government offices, both federal and state, the change is easy to see. Before, most routine operations required some small "gratifications" before they could go ahead. In many, probably most offices, this is no longer true. Things work as they should, without bribes.

As just one example, many state governments have mostly eliminated bribes from the driver's license operations. It used to be that you could hardly get anything done without some kind of bribe. There was one price for a standard license with a driving test, but another, higher of course, without the test, and you knew that you'd never be allowed to pass the test. Vision or health problems could be overlooked with still another bribe.

But many have now streamlined operations *almost* without bribes. The rules are published, the required documents are listed, and provided you meet specifications, you get your driver's license the same day. The change is revolutionary.

On the other hand, if you have a matter at a busy police station, you will still be constantly assaulted for *gratifications* to get your case handled on time. Lots of luck if you're poor!

Little by little, the government's top levels are imposing reasonable rules on the bottom levels to eliminate the bribes. With exception of traffic patrol bribes and other police matters, which is a self-preserving system with a long tradition, they seem to be successful.

Did all this happen in the US, too?

Of course! There are differences in culture in the two countries, but one thing is the same: politics and "public service" attract many opportunistic persons who have no qualms about self enrichment *if only they can get away with it!* At least, that's the way I see it.

Historians will tell anyone that wants to listen about periods of blatant corruption in US federal and many state governments. Thoroughly corrupt politicians and police were the norm in many American cities in the nineteenth century, and persisted well into the twentieth century.

It's also true that politics also attracts some highly motivated, idealistic people who can make excellent public servants. That happens on both sides of the border. But it's not easy to distinguish the two, and to be perfectly frank, probably all are some kind of mixture of both extremes. We'd even be afraid to have completely idealistic leaders who can't make pragmatic and opportunistic compromises when this is necessary. After all, politics is the art of accomplishing practical results in a real world, and conditions are never ideal.

The various US publics that faced these problems decided they would no longer be tolerated. The nature of the people that became politicians and police didn't change. The rules changed.

In the same way, Mexico is changing the rules. Progress is evident. There's a long way to go. But Mexico will get there, just as the US did. Corruption of these sorts will never be eliminated, but it can be controlled. And it will be controlled.

I should admit that there are many, both in Mexico and the US, that don't think there's much difference now in the two countries, except that major corruption is better hidden in the US than in Mexico. I don't know. I hope not, but I can't be sure. The fact that you are always actively bothered by drug sellers on many public streets in and around Washington, D.C., at least suggests there is a hidden problem.

Ways to Promote Corruption

The Prohibition Amendment (18th Amendment to the US Constitution) prohibited the manufacture, transportation, and sale of alcoholic beverages from 1920 to 1933 in the US. Although characterized as "a noble experiment" by US president Herbert Hoover, it was, simply, a failure. In practice, it did not lower consumption of alcohol: rather it promoted the use of "hard liquor," which was more profitable for bootleggers. In addition, it proved to be a bonanza to organized crime, which grew to unprecedented wealth in the US.

Mexicans tend to believe that enforcement of current US laws against marijuana, cocaine, heroin, and other prohibited drugs is doing the same. These drugs are certainly more available now in the US than ever before, in small towns as well as in the large cities. But the organized crime that thrives on drug operations is obviously having a large and noxious effect on all phases of political, police, and military affairs in Mexico.

The Drug Problem

It's no secret that Mexico is caught in the middle of the American drug problem. The US has the largest consumption of drugs, and now even the majority, despite the law, doesn't believe it immoral or dangerous to smoke an occasional "joint" or "reefer."

It's US policy to vigorously enforce the ban on the use of the illegal drugs. This immediately establishes a price support for the illegal drugs. Production increased in several countries, and large-scale criminal organization grew from the profits of dealing with the drugs.

Mexico certainly didn't have a significant drug problem a decade or two ago. Just finding the substances in small towns and cities wasn't easy in those days.

But Mexico was the one logical route into the US market, and as a result, the drug trade grew in Mexico. Even the opium poppy was grown as a cash crop, and now campesinos everywhere know the techniques for harvesting the opium resin. The quantities of all the drugs that cross the border into the US, the great majority in transit from other countries, are gigantic, and profits are gigantic.

But of course, it's all illegal. The effect on Mexico at all levels has been disastrous. There's lots of money to subvert, and it's actively used at all levels. The effect on government, military, police, general security of the public is a disaster. Where wages are low, there's really nothing like the money from the drug trade.

But it's even worse. Since it's to the advantage of many to have drugs available for sale, the sheer quantity of drugs floating around Mexico is now tremendous. As a result, it's available in large quantities everywhere. Now Mexican kids everywhere are being seduced by drugs.

Is there anything good about corruption?

You can hardly find a major street intersection in Mexico City in which you aren't offered chewing gum, Kleenex, flowers, red distress flannels,...hundreds of things. Every large city is plagued with itinerants selling foods, electronic goods, candies, potato chips, music cassettes, video cassettes, and almost anything that can fit on a sidewalk or street.

Now let's take the specific problem of Mexico City. With its population now about 20 million people, the sheer number of street vendors is astounding. And this presents a problem (many problems, really, but just one I want to mention here). Since it is basically an illegal occupation in Mexican government eyes, it has to be *spontaneous*. But can you imagine the problems in a wholly spontaneous street vendor scene? Nobody could depend on his vending spot on any given day. You'd have turf wars. Anarchy and disorganization would rear its ugly head.

So because of its very need for organization, Mexico City has organized its street scene. People now *buy* their selling places, or they *rent* them, and there is a *pseudopolice* force that enforces the contract. There are vendors, organizers and leaders of vendors, higher authorities in the scheme, etc. The fact is, that this illegal system is completely organized by district, and there is, of course, a city-wide superstructure. Everybody supposes, and some say they know for sure, that there are political leaders who take their profits from the system.

That is to say, we have a safer city because of the corruption. And we certainly don't want the city without that form of corruption. Do we support this corruption? It exists because people buy things from the street sellers, some out of pity, most out of convenience. But fortunes are made by this corruption.

Now let's go on to bigger things. The reason Mexico has progressed so much more than its neighbors to the south (I mean, virtually almost all of Latin America!) is that it has had stability in government. Because of that stability, business was able to develop, and as a result, jobs were created. It could (and should) have been much better: more development, more honesty, and more jobs. Still, by Latin American standards, it's an amazing success story, admired by all who understand the alternatives.

We have certainly done well with our American system of government. But for the Latins, the Mexican system really functioned well. But it was, by any standards, corrupt. As a matter of fact, in this case, corruption was part of the glue that held it together.

What I have said is that corruption is highly underrated in words in this lovely country. Almost all Mexicans publicly abhor corruption. It is a nasty word. But is actually accepted by almost everybody, including yours truly. The problem lies in keeping it under control.

And that, my Gringo friend, is what you'll be faced with. You will find corruption. You will need to live with it. And with your Gringo background, that won't be easy; and with your Gringo face, it may even be dangerous (you could be an excellent scapegoat or an easy mark). But you have no choice. You must live with it.

Canadians Different from Americans?

It's interesting that Mexicans can take different approaches to Americans and Canadians on the matter of bribes for obtaining legal permits, etc. They know it is difficult and very illegal for the Americans to pay bribes. But they can consider that the Canadians, being from a "much more reasonable country," can recognize the bribe system as more rational and more normal in the world. They are perfectly capable of insisting on bribes more directly from Canadians than from Americans.

That's the Mexican view. But it's wrong. Bribery is taken seriously in the US, but to all accounts, it's much more serious in Canada. Canadian firms reportedly do lose contracts because they don't pay the bribes many countries' officials require. Even with NAFTA, Mexican companies have problems in Mexico.

4

MONEY IS A COMMON DENOMINATOR

You may once have thought of yourself as "poor," or "thrifty," or "living on a tight budget." Here you might learn just what that means! You need to understand that on a personal basis, money is much scarcer in Mexico than in the US. As a result, idealism of a certain kind , common in the US, is much scarcer in Mexico. I'll help you with a few rules for transactions in this country.

Now let's get down to brass tacks. This is another theme that you must understand to live in Mexico.

Some Background

Mexico is a successful country in terms of industrial development. Its development proceeds quite rapidly in most years, and its industrial infrastructure is quite large. According to the NAFTA studies, Mexico's Gross Domestic Product (GDP) growth rate averaged 2.0 % compared with 2.5 % for the US from 1984 to 1995. For most years the growth was higher than population growth.

Still, since the population growth of Mexico is so great, the benefit is felt very little. The average person will never advance very much as long as the population continues to grow as fast as it does. Real wages can never increase very much until the GDP grows much faster than the population, an almost impossible feat for Mexico as it is now. As a matter of fact, there are limits to the sustained growth of economies, and these limits are much smaller than the limits to growth of populations.

So, in Mexico, it's easy to see that: Money is important!

Well, that's not news! But in the US we have lots of people who aren't rich say they are just doing what they want to do, without regard for money. I was taught to get a full liberal arts education without considering what I'd do for a living afterwards.

And I know some of my classmates actually did. Frankly, I admire them. But the fact is, at least in the US in times past, you could always make a living somehow. Enough jobs were available, and you could at least earn barely enough to live. (Still, I admit that most of my classmates and I did honestly think a bit of how we would survive after graduation.)

In Mexico, you need to know that that's hardly an option for an ordinary person. Here there simply aren't enough jobs to go around, and the available ones hardly pay enough to live decently. You need to worry, unless, that is, you're born so rich it doesn't matter, or you can take over the family business.

I suspect it's getting that way in the US.

There are People with Money in Mexico

It's obvious that there are plenty of people with money in Mexico. Unfortunately, they are more visible than in the US and Canada. They contrast much more with the rest of us.

I much admire people and families who got their money by applying the Puritan virtues, though I personally don't know of many of them. There certainly are Mexican rich who deserve their money. But most

Mexicans tend to doubt that they earned their money. Still, they are tolerated quite nicely.

If you are doing business in Mexico, you will most likely be associated with these people. Others most likely don't have the resources to work with you.

Middle Level People

Workers in the US, especially the broad spectrum of white collar and scientific workers, have traditionally been able to live without constantly scrounging for money in second and part-time jobs.

But let's be real. The recent *thinning down* underway in the US brought the harsh light of day to many who used to be comfortable. Still, there are many more available jobs in the US and Canada than in Mexico. There's even room to import workers in some fields, such as computer scientists and other brain workers. In Mexico, there's always an excess of workers, even in these fields.

Mexican wages are low. Government workers are not well paid. Private industry pays its workers even less. Wages are almost never living wages as in Canada and the US. To maintain what you consider a decent standard of living in Mexico, you normally need to have something else going: part-time job, consulting work, whatever. As an example, most teachers I know at all levels have some kind of second job or other source of income.

Poor People

I needn't say anything more about the rest of the population. Most are simply poor, with all that suggests. It's obvious that they form a much larger percentage of the population of Mexico than the poor of the US.

Money in Practice

Let's take a closer look at money in the Mexican scheme. Since here in Mexico we don't have much money, we must admit that money is important in our lives. In the US we can pretend, but that's not even possible here. The people who are rich and cultured know very well that despite all else, the only thing that keeps them different from the rest is simply the money they have or control.

There are even special events, uncommon in the US, that emphasize the problem. In 1986 and 1994, the Mexican currency was devalued by 50%. That immediately meant that all wage earners took a 50% cut in real wages in both cases.

Now, that gets your attention. Can you imagine the consequences of a 50% across the board reduction of wages in the US? Things like this have happened several times to the Mexican wage earner in the last few decades. Real prices of virtually everything are affected. Locally produced foods are least affected, but they are affected; and transnational goods are most affected. As the US and Mexican economies become more united, the more drastic these problems will be.

Transactions

I will direct your attention now to transactions. I talk about transactions in the general sense. Every transaction you will make in Mexico will probably involve money. If it's a sale, or it's a contract, it will obviously involve money. If it's a social function, money will play its part. If it's a government license, there will probably be unofficial money involved.

It used to be a relatively easy game for foreigners. They had more money to spend and apparently more desire to risk their money than the Mexicans. But the Mexicans with money had it stashed in the US or some other country, where it could be safe (and, where, of course, it could help develop the US economy). The Americans couldn't hide their money, because all the structures in the US encouraged them to show and use what they had, and anyway, it was not considered evil to have money.

The Mexicans had other problems. It seems incongruent, but there was a strongly "socialist" cast to official government policy. Peoples with wealth used to be classified as wicked because they had it. Officially they were actually expected to give it up voluntarily to the government.

Of course, these populist governments traditionally looked for ways to take it away from them, so people were long accustomed to hiding what they had. They hid it in other countries. They were called "vendepatrias," which means they sold out their country. But they were used to that. They had no idealistic drive towards the poverty which the government tried to impose.

It's interesting to note that the government actually did take a lot of money away from people in quite shameless ways. One of the most bald-faced was to convert all dollar accounts into pesos. Of course, the conversion rate was so low that the effect was to confiscate half of the money. Needless to say, this even affected idealistic Americans and other innocents. I know of one person who took his United Nations pension in a lump sum and invested it in a dollar account in Mexico, and thereby had half of it expropriated. Of course, Mexicans know about these things. Rich Mexicans had *their* money in the US and Europe, where it was much safer.

But with the new free trade agreement, the government has signaled that it wants the money back in Mexico, and it set up guarantees that encourage its repatriation. So a large part of the Mexican money is now back, and *it is your competition*. If there's money to be made, there will be Mexican money available to compete.

This leads me to offer some practical advice. I'm really not the best person for this because obviously I haven't had much experience with large quantities of money. I haven't made my bundle. My kids will have to earn their own. But I can suggest a few things.

Evaluate every transaction

By "every transaction" I mean *every transaction*. If it's important to you, the person on the other end will know it, and will probably expect some recognition (money, of course) on your part. If you need a license, apart from the fees, the person who will finally issue it will probably expect a gratification. You need to know what it's worth, and you need to know how much you are willing to pay. You may even be able to talk openly with him about the problem. And you need to understand the risks you'll run with your own country's laws, where such gratifications may well be considered as illegal and certainly cannot be deducted as business expenses.

If you don't have the stomach, hire somebody who does

You must deal in the real world if you expect to accomplish anything. This means you must squarely face the issues. If a bribe is called for, and you don't handle bribes well (as I don't) get somebody who does. If he's American, maybe somebody raised in another big city, perhaps New York City, would be able to help. There are certainly many Mexicans with experience you can turn to. But be aware that your intermediary will have to be sufficiently dishonest that you will even have trouble trusting him.

Evaluate alternate paths

From personal experience, I can say that people in the smaller cities are more visibly dishonest than in Mexico City, although the matter is quite visible everywhere. The Mexican proverb is "Little town, big Hell!" (*Pueblo chico, infierno grande!*). (There is a Mexican saying for any situation you can name!) You will be more likely to succeed if you take these realities into account.

For example, if you are trying to set up a business, in a really bad case you may need to offer the official a piece of the action. However, this will probably be fatal in any case. You really don't want him as partner, but if his stake is involved, he may go the extra mile to make the project really work. You can do little against local governmental opposition, and this usually means the local officials need to be on your side. How to put them on your side? Your ingenuity. But sorry to say, it usually involves money.

Speak the Language of Love

- even when you know it's lust. To a traffic cop on the make, you talk about his tip for a coke, even when the money involved doesn't correspond to the cost of a coke. To a customs agent, talk about the noble effect your new equipment will have on the job status of the entire country. It's part of the ritual. Courtesy in everything!

The Low End

Now, for two views of the money problem, one from the low end, and one from the high end. From the low end, you will recognize that a lot of small mistakes are made in stores, banks, movies, whatever. The mistake, of course, is never in the interest of the client. Where I live, in one period, there wasn't a single bank without this problem: "What? The change isn't just right? Why, you're right! I charged you the commission twice, didn't I. I'm sorry! Here it is!"

This is petty theft, but it used to be rampant. Foreigners as well as Mexicans who don't pay attention to details always suffer. In my experience, it is highly organized so that the different employees all profit from it. Still, Mexico is truly changing fast. I haven't seen nearly as much in recent years.

The High End

Now for the high end. There is an elaborate system of public offerings for government purchases to ensure that the government gets a good deal. The system involves prequalification of firms who are allowed to bid, proof of financial soundness, sealed bids (lots of luck on that one) and other safeguards. In short, there's a complete open system, with strong theoretical underpinning, that guarantees the government will pay reasonable prices for what it purchases.

In the past it was obvious that there was an inordinate amount of money being made on sales to the government. There are now such stringent checks on the process that it is no longer obvious how money could exchange hands in the process. But there's always the suspicion.

The Bottom Line

As a practical matter, you must be aware that there is no free lunch in Mexico. The system is not set up to guarantee you a profit. It is set up to pass money into other hands, normally without killing the beneficent source. They know about the goose with the golden eggs. You do too.

If you're a businessman, you need to figure out how to live in the system. It won't be easy, but you can probably do it. If you're not a businessman, it won't be so hard.

A Sidelight on Tipping

When you go to a hotel in the US, you assume that the employees are paid adequately for their work. You do give tips for many services, but you don't feel that it's that important a thing. Most Americans don't even thinking of leaving tips for the people who clean their hotel rooms and make their beds.

In Mexico, this is really important money. Almost all hotel employees actually need supplements to their wages, if they actually have wages. That is to say, you should leave tips in your hotel room as you leave, just as you tip a bellboy or a waiter in a restaurant.

How much should you tip? In taxis, a small, tip, proportional to the charge, is reasonable and well accepted for good service, but it's not necessary. In restaurants, the percentages used in the US are fine. On the other hand, for bellboys, porters, cleaning personnel and the life, it's your call, but you need to consider that these people actually do depend on your tips for a living.

5

PASS THE ENCHILADAS—STUFFED PEPPERS—GORDITOS—POZOLE—HUANZONTLES—...

Not to mention Mixiote, real Guacamole, Tostadas,...I could go on forever. This is not diet land. Nor is it for the unadventurous. Eating is one of the pleasures of Mexico. Almost everybody overdoes it, and so will you. There's more excitement in a month of good Mexican home cooking than you'll find in a lifetime in the US.

Some people will say that Americans eat to live, but that Mexicans live to eat. There's something to that. To me, Mexican food is so infinitely varied, with such fine flavors and textures, that eating is a distinct pleasure. By comparison, though I really do enjoy them, standard American foods just don't ring a bell.

In the greater scheme of things, Mexican food may well be the most varied in the world. Restaurants tend to have things you expect, because they live by tempting you to known things, but even restaurants in Mexico normally have a good variety of dishes. But Mexican cultural and biological diversity have promoted an extremely wide variety of dishes on the table. In particular, home cooking in Mexico, hardly even available to tourists, is a remarkable art in Mexico, and it is extremely varied.

Let me whet your appetite about what's here.

Tortillas

When the Spanish conquistadores arrive in Mexico, ladies were making tortillas. It's done by hand: flattening a ball of corn meal dough and heating it on a flat surface until it's ready to eat. (They aren't made by frying.) During a meal, somebody will, to this day, heat tortillas during a meal so you never have to eat a cold one.

Tortillas are still the staple. Whereas many Americans need bread at every meal, Mexicans need tortillas. They are now usually made by machine and heated on the stove or in the microwave oven for a meal, but in general, they are about the same as in the old days.

We all develop our eating habits as kids, and all Mexican kids depend on tortillas. All Mexicans expect tortillas with a meal. Without them it doesn't seem like a meal! Frankly, every Mexican can distinguish between ordinary tortillas and really great tortillas, although we poor Gringos normally can hardly even tell the good ones from the bad.

There have to be tortillas on the table. You can roll them up and eat them as is, or you can put something inside. I'm not going to describe them more because you're going to see them and see how they are used. The only things that's impossible is...not using them in a meal. They even form the internal ingredients of many foods, and there are many uses for dried tortillas. You'll see! (And if you don't, you'll know you're doing something terribly wrong!)

Fruit

Mexico has fine fresh fruit all year around, and it's inexpensive. I know people who cross the border, go first to the market, and load up on all fresh fruit they can carry, and just nibble all the time they are in Mexico.

Here you can do it all the time. And you know it's healthy for you! No more vitamin pills. Here you can get your vitamins the best way, by eating fresh fruit all day long.

What fruit do they have? Everything they have in the US and Canada. Even things like kiwi, grown locally or imported from New Zealand. Citrus: oranges, lemons, limes, grapefruit, *limas* (more like oranges, but green, with a bland flavor). All you can want, all cheap, all year round, though of course it's all better and cheaper in season. Apples and pears, both native and imported. Excellent bananas, in three or four varieties, all year round: regular "chiquitas," big frying bananas (*plátano macho*, which I won't translate), pink bananas, tiny extra good bananas (*dominicanos*). Peaches and plums, grapes, watermelons, muskmelons. You name it. Not many cherries, hardly any cranberries, no Concord grapes that I've seen, but really almost everything you find in supermarkets in the US..

But of course, they have tropical fruits too. Native tropicals are papayas, all year round. Mangos in season; there is no finer fruit in Mexico than "*mango de manila*." Chirimoyas. Pineapples (they came from Mexico). Guavas that are really excellent. And there are other things you may not recognize: *zapote, nísperas* (loquats), prickley pears (*tunas*),...

Enjoy! This is a luxury you'll never have farther north.

Vegetables

A lot of our vegetables come from Mexico originally, and others from the Americas in general. Corn, squash, chili peppers, and beans were the main diet before the Spanish arrived. The saying was, "People are made of corn." And they were, and are. Corn was what allowed Tenochtitlán, the prehispanic predecessor to Mexico City, to exist. But of course, squash and beans always accompanied the corn in the field. Potatoes aren't big in Mexico, except maybe as chips; potatoes are native to South America, not to Mexico.

You'll enjoy seeing vegetables in the markets. Most you'll recognize, but you'll find varieties that you don't see in the US. You'll also probably note that many taste better, just because they are grown in more natural ways than in the US.

Mole (You say "MOH-lay." There's no translation.)

I can't believe I postponed *mole* so long in this chapter. I am simply addicted to it. It's that black nasty-looking pasty stuff you see in the markets, dished out by the kilo, or sold bottled in supermarkets. To me, *mole* is *the* Mexican food. I must have some every so often or I think I'm back in Gringoland, where food isn't really food. Since it's a festive food, you tend to see it when you have company or parties. Now you know why Mexicans welcome strangers so readily? Or why they like parties? Can you image Americans wanting to have company just so they can have some of that wonderful stuff?

What is *mole?* It's a very complex mixture of chocolate, chili peppers, and some twenty other spices. Most families have an aunt, someplace, that makes the *mole* for the family, but it's usually an old-fashioned aunt, and her daughters aren't bothering to keep the tradition. That's what's happening in my Mexican family. But now you can buy half a dozen varieties in large markets, and you can't even imagine an organized market that doesn't sell several kinds. It is simply indispensable for Mexican cooking.

When you go to a Mexican restaurant, you are liable to get an unnamed black sauce on things when you least expect it. Of course, if it's a good restaurant it will offer *mole* with chicken and with many other things with *mole*, and so you're prepared. But it's the flavor that eventually traps you. There is no other sauce in the world with a flavor like that. I won't describe it. I'll just tell you to try it a few times, and if you don't like it after a few tries, I will be thoroughly surprised. (Do you know anybody who really liked sushi the first time around?) I know we are all tied to the flavors we learned in childhood, but if you can't get by that enough to enjoy a good *mole*, well, you've got a real problem.

Now don't get me wrong. You can't like all *moles*. There are many of them, and they are all a little different. Some may be too hot (*picante*) for you. Some have mixtures of spices that are a little strong for me, even. But as a general rule, I like almost all of them, and I can't believe you won't. Just try them, as many varieties as you can.

And if your servant's family makes *mole* at home, you really have a treat brewing. That will be the real stuff. And they can make it a bit different for you, more or less sweet, more or less hot, with or without a certain spice...That's special.

I am addicted to the wonderful flavors of *moles*. It's a psychological addiction I admit. A real chocolate addict might get relief from it. I suppose you could develop a physical addiction by eating *mole* every day. (I'll volunteer for the experiment.)

I should add that there's also a green *mole (mole verde)*. This doesn't have chocolate in it, and it's completely different in appearance and taste, made with green tomatillos. It's good, too, but despite the name, it's not at all like the chocolate-based mole.

Picante: Hot Stuff

I have to talk about hot stuff (*picante*) in the food. Chile peppers are mostly hot in Mexico (probably the only one that's not hot is the ordinary green pepper that we have in the US, called *pimiento morrón* by some). People are raised on hot foods in Mexico. So you tend to find hot peppers in almost everything that's not sweet, and people add hot sauce or hot powder to almost any fresh fruit. Other countries have even hotter foods, such as India and Bolivia, but none can beat Mexican foods for taste.

If you see a schoolboy on the street eat popcorn, he'll always add hot sauce first. Or if he eats an apple, or a mango, or any other fruit, he'll always sprinkle it with powdered hot chile powder first.

You can see that people of all ages are used to finding hot in their foods. But they don't tend to occur in all foods, and in many they are optional. As an example, a typical *mole* is pretty hot. Still, if it's prepared for you and your Gringo ways, it probably won't be very hot. Since most Mexican families have a member or two who don't like things too hot, there's usually hot sauce on the table for everyone to use to his own taste. In any case, if you see chile seeds, go slowly.

Over time you should develop a little tolerance, if not a taste, for hot things. I did. I do like it, within reason. It's just one of the limiting factors to my eating in Mexico. Whenever I'm eating out, whether it's a family or a restaurant, I let it be known that I don't want any or much *picante*. Mexicans try to please, and usually they hold the *picante* on my dishes.

Mexicans tend to believe that hot is healthy, and that lack of hot is probably not, and some scientific studies support that view. Some recognize that *picante* is irritating. But most feel that, for example, that *picante* used to protect against polio, and there are reports that chiles have enzymes which help the digestion of complex bean dishes. So the reflex is usually to include some hot in a meal.

Bread

If you're like me, you probably never had real bread before you came to Mexico. Good bread is a luxury that is mostly missing in the US Here you can have fine bread, really fine bread, at every meal. It's another way in which the developed world is more underdeveloped than the underdeveloped world.

How to go about it? Just go to the local bakery. There are several in every neighborhood. Note that there are perhaps 50 different pastries available at any time, but they're not the soft French varieties. The nomenclature varies tremendously, but some unsweetened breads are *bolillos y teleras*. In my house the custom is to eat sweetened breads at breakfast, and some of these are called *conchas and bigotes*. Of course there are doughnuts (*donas*) and other pastries.

Go ahead! Be a glutton! You'll forgive yourself.

Tamales

All Mexican foods are regional. Even tortillas are different in different parts of the country. You see this especially clearly in things like *tamales*.

The main *tamales* that I know are the *ranchero* and the ordinary *tamales*. The *rancheros* are wrapped in banana leaves. They're the ones that most appeal to the Gringo taste. Ordinary tamales are wrapped in corn husks. (What you usually see in the US are the normal ones.) Contents of the ordinary ones vary normally between pork, chicken, and beef, but there are also sweet ones.

But *tamales* also vary by region. On the Yucatán Peninsula you'll get gigantic things you won't recognize. But they are also fine.

And there are also specialized *tamales* for certain saints' days and other events, that are different from the others.

In any case, you can't go wrong with *tamales*.

Mixiote

I've mentioned *mole*, which is my absolute favorite. But that's not the only remarkable Mexican flavor. Another is *mixiote* ("mee-shee-OH-tay"). This is relatively hard to find: there are no basic pastes on sale in markets. If your maid is from the right part of the country, she can make it, or she has relatives who do. It's also available in restaurants, and in roadside fast food stands. I can't tell you much about them, however.

But you should know that in the *absolute genuine mixiote* different from normal Mexican customs, is a male specialty. That is to say, in mixiote country, it's the father of the household who makes it. It's not a trivial matter, and it takes the better part of a day, so it's something that's done only for big party days. I can't tell you the ingredients, but I can tell you that it is some fine eating! You won't regret trying that one.

Pozole

You'll run across *pozole* ("poh-SOH-lay") on special ceremonial days. In my Mexican family we eat pozole on New Year's Eve, Easter, and special occasions like some birthdays. What is it? Again, it varies around the country, but the central ingredient is hominy! In my family it must have some pork, some chicken, and some beef. It's served with lots of chopped radishes and chopped lettuce, as well as Mexican oregano (almost the same as American oregano), chopped onion, and lemon squeezed on it all.

This is another non-subtle dish, but one that satisfies.

Huanzontles

See if you can get someone to fix you *huanzontles*. You probably won't find them in restaurants, certainly not in tourist restaurants, but they are fine eating. Unexpected, but fine…

What are they? They are a plant that somewhat reminds you of very thick asparagus fern, but they have a fine flavor. They are prepared differently by different cooks, but in my family they have cheese tucked throughout the leafy branches, and they have a crusty coating cooked on, and they are served with *mole* or tomato sauce, or even by themselves.

When you see them, you won't know exactly how to eat them. But I'll tell you. You pick them up with your hands, and you string them through your teeth.

The flavor is excellent. The texture is unusual but very agreeable.

Would you Believe, *Smut?*

One of the neat, unique foods in Mexico is: smut! *Huitlacoche* (Weet-lah-COH-chay), also called *cuitalacoche*, is what corn farmers in the US used to fear, called corn smut. This is a black fungus that grows on the corn and if it spreads too far, it can ruin a crop.

But it's a neat food. You can have it in smut soup (*sopa de huitlacoche*), smut *empanadas* (*huitlacoche* folded into soft tortillas, which are folded over, sealed, and fried) and many other ways. You can buy it in most markets, and you can even buy it canned in the supermarket.

I recommend you try it. It doesn't have a nice name in English, but you'll probably like it if you don't think of its name.

Birría, and Others

There are certainly plenty of other dishes. Just be open to the idea, and you will have no regrets, although you may end up a few pounds overweight. Let me just name a few things to look out for: *birría,* stuffed peppers in all their variations, tacos in all their variations, Swiss enchiladas (enchiladas that aren't hot, usually with tomato sauce), enchiladas in general, and there are many others. The variety in Mexico is endless.

For the Really Adventurous

Mexico has a number of traditional foods that seem adventurous to Americans and Canadians. These include a variety of grasshoppers and larvae that are prepared in one way or another and enjoyed as delicacies. They are just a small remnant of pre-Hispanic foods that don't necessarily appeal to Europeans of that age or this.

You most often find these things at regional fairs, and sometimes you see them in central markets. Just keep your eyes open. You'll find them, and you can try them.

Hamburgers

You say, *hamburguesas?* In Mexico? With all that magnificent real food all over?

Well, I must admit, I like a good hamburger now and then. I know it has more fat than is appropriate, but it also has greens and tomatoes. Junk food? I don't think so.

And anyway, if you're going to limit yourself to fitness foods, you're probably not going to eat much regular Mexican food.

Just know this: MacDonald's and Burger King and other burger makers are now found all over the country. Whenever you want a hamburger, you can get one. I admit that good pickles are rare here, but you might start enjoying hot sauce on your burger as do most Mexicans.

The same is true for fried chicken, too, and other American fast foods can be found in most cities.

6

EATING RULES FOR FOREIGNERS

Mexican food is certainly superb, but you do have to know what and how to eat. How about eating on the street where everything smells and looks and tastes even better than indoors? Well, you can do it. Here I'm going to try to help you keep healthy while you indulge yourself.

What and how to eat! That is the question.

Are you going to stay in Mexico full time for a long time, or are you coming and going for months at a time, or are you just in and out. Your eating strategy depends on whether you can afford to develop a resistance to the native bugs.

If you come to Mexico only for short periods, don't take chances. It's not worth it. Eat at home or in good restaurants, brush your teeth with bottled mineral water, and don't ever, ever, eat on the street, nor think of eating salads unless you know the raw things are rinsed in water treated with iodine. (Colloidal silver and other antiseptics are sold in all large grocery stores.) That still leaves you more fine eating than you'll have almost anywhere.

But if you are going to spend more time in Mexico for a while, say months at a time, you can adopt a different strategy. You want your system to adapt so you can eat really well. Brush your teeth with tap water, but don't drink the water. Eat things that are well cooked on the street. Eat salads with care.

Whatever you do, don't drink the water!

You need to know that water in most cities and towns is not processed at all, although this is changing fast. It's distinctly dangerous for those of us without defenses. It's not just the simple runs (diarrhea) that will get you. There are hepatitis and amebas and *Giardia lamblia* lurking there. Just don't take chances.

Drink your beer or your coke or your bottled water. But be careful with bottled water from the street, which may be rebottled (tap water placed in recycled bottled water bottles). Normally I'm in favor of buying from the little man, but I buy my bottled water from stores that would be hurt if they handled rebottled water.

All this is a good excuse to drink coke or beer, or bottled water, but it's a valid excuse. They say the water in Mexico City and some other large cities is chlorinated, and it may well be. All my relatives drink it without problems, but it always gives me problems. I suppose it's just not chlorinated enough. It's obvious that I'm not yet strong enough. You won't be, either.

Of course, good hotels that cater to tourists will process their own water. I've never heard of a person with problems from water from the top tourist hotels. But even there, it wouldn't hurt to indulge yourself like a Mexican and drink only bottled things or prepared fruit ades that are served in good tourist restaurants. As a whole, Mexicans just don't drink water from the tap. They don't feel the need since they have so many other better tasting drinks available.

You also need to know that simple active-carbon water filtration systems don't provide protection. They remove many things, but they can't be depended on to totally remove the microorganisms that cause problems, despite the advertising you may see. Our family solution is to have two giant pots of well boiled water, one of which can be boiling at any time.

Eat on the Street?

Different parts of Mexico have different names for street food. Where I live, they are called *garnachas*. *Garnachas* are a real treat.

You do need to be careful. I've known young traveling Americans who only eat in markets or on the streets because the food really does taste better there. You can easily be seduced by the wonderful food odors on any street corner or in any market, and the flavors are, if anything, even better than the smells.

Should you eat on the street? Well, I do, but only selectively. With time you can distinguish what is safe and what isn't. Hard tortillas are generally safe, as are all sorts of cooked things. Bottled drinks: beer, mineral water, all sorts of soft drinks are OK.

Raw vegetables generally are not OK. Even if they are washed, the water is probably not potable. Hygiene is a problem in most places on the street.

You need to know Mexico has trichinosis, though much less than in the recent past. In practice, this means that when you eat pork, be extremely careful. Eat only well-cooked pork. *Carnitas* are bits of pork, fried in an open pot until well done. They are a real treat. But make sure they are well done. I know a person with epilepsy as a result of eating *carnitas* in a party when she was a child. It's a high price to pay. Accept *carnitas* in a home situation rather than a roadside stand, but even then only with great care.

Just be careful. No lettuce or fresh salads in doubtful areas. No uncooked sauces. No uncooked foods. Nothing from people who are obviously not concerned with hygiene.

Experience on the Street

You can learn by experience. I always figured that corn on the cob should be dangerous if bought on the street (the only place you can buy it), not for the corn but for the mayonnaise and cheese used on it. But I'm a habitual corn-on-the-cob-on-the-street eater, and I've never had a problem with it. I recommend it to you. Eat away!

By the way, Mexicans use mayonnaise on their corn-on-the-cob, not butter like most Americans. Try it. You may well prefer it. Mexicans in some places prefer corn-on-the-cob charred over a grill; it's worth trying, but you probably won't prefer that.

I always figured stuffed peppers on the street should be safe. They are all cooked well, aren't they? I dearly love stuffed peppers, even with the excess of "hot" they usually have. But I've never eaten stuffed peppers on the street without suffering afterwards. It would seem to be the hygiene, somehow, but maybe it's just the excess "hots" that they have.

There are plenty of other things available that shouldn't cause problems. The *tamales*, both the "rancheros" (big ones in banana leaves) and ordinary ones (in corn husks) are safe in almost all cases, except that some of the ordinary ones have red food colors added which we, as Gringos, assume not to be safe.

But just don't ever eat uncooked things on the street, except things that come protected by a peel, such as tangerines. Lettuce and hot sauces on the street are out (since the sauces probably contain unboiled water). Your rule on the street is that you only eat things that are purified by fire. And you avoid things that are good media for cultivating unfriendly microscopic bugs.

And never buy food prepared by a lady with a baby. She probably never washes her hands. Enough said!

What's Left?

So what does that leave? Well, hold the lettuce and you find excellent *tacos al pastor* everywhere. These have bits of meat in a soft tortilla. And hard tortillas with things on top, called tostadas in some parts, simply can't be beat.

Sandwiches, almost always of ham, made with sliced white bread, are available everywhere and for me, at least, have proven completely safe. You might want to open them to take out that fiery slice of pepper that comes in most of them. I don't see them as very pleasurable, but they certainly can solve a hunger problem. As a matter of fact, many Mexicans consider them Gringo food, not very good but sufficient to satisfy the needs of a Gringo.

Tortas are somewhat better. *Tortas* are the same as sandwiches except that they are made with a large bun, opened or sliced in half. They, too, often have ham, but there's a considerable variety of them out there. I've never heard of any health problem with sandwiches or *tortas*.

Unlike sandwiches, tortas are available in a very wide variety of styles and fillings. The rule for tortas is: *you can make a torta of anything that can fit in the bun.* Typical *tortas* have ham or chicken, but you also find *tortas* of sausage, potato, pork chop, fried or boiled egg, and the like. *Tortas* are wholesome and they all taste good.

Eating at Home or in Restaurants

Eating at home or in good tourist restaurants changes the picture. You control the sanitation at home, and you trust the restaurant. So there are hardly any limits to what you can enjoy.

Still, there are a few problems. At home you must make sure your maid follows your ideas of sanitation. That includes washing hands before handling foods and after going to the bathroom, boiling water, and soaking greens in some kind of sterilizing solution. She may never have done this for anybody, and she's never known she could suffer from the lack. And she may not, because her defenses are stronger than yours.

Hot (*picante*) things can give problems. Almost everything can be prepared with none, a bit, or a lot of *picante*. The reflex is almost always: a lot! You need to change the maid's reflex to your own preference.

Healthy Eating

Here I'm sure you know more than I do; I've lived in Mexico too long. Normal Mexican food is not low fat nor low sodium nor low sugar The fact is, I've lived in Mexico so long and I've eaten so much traditional Mexican food that I'd probably have problems adjusting to a healthier diet with less fat, meat and salt and more fiber such as you probably eat.

For that, I'll probably check out earlier than you. I've accepted that.

You'll just have to use your creativity to figure out how to eat healthy in Mexico. I'm sure it can be done, and I'm even sure it is the way of the future. In five years there will be an emphasis on healthy foods here, low in animal fats, etc.

It's fairly easy to avoid animal fats, except for what comes with meat. You can always ask for the fat to be removed before cooking. But avoiding fats altogether is hard in Mexico. Many, maybe most, foods are fried in one way or another or deep fried.

Actually, cooking oils are much like in the US, from corn, sesame, and others. Very little use is made of lard, and when it is used, it's advertised. It's more expensive than vegetable oils for cooking.

You don't eat pork? That's probably not a problem. People who sell or serve you food usually know if it contains pork. Just ask. *Carne de puerco* or *carne de cerdo* is pork. *Carne de res* is beef, and *pollo* and *carne de pollo* is chicken.

Low salt diet? That's a hard one. In a household, salt can be controlled if you make your needs known. Since many restaurant foods are prepared in bulk in advanced, it may not be possible in restaurants, unless you're in a health food (often vegetarian) or kosher restaurant. On the other hand, many things are prepared without any salt: there's no *pinch of salt* in most

Mexican recipes of bread and pastries, and table salt is not even furnished in most catered banquets.

Other dietary problems may be hard to control. Still, there are many vegetarian and health restaurants in most of the country, and there are even a few kosher restaurants. There are fewer additives in foods, since most are prepared fresh. It may not be harder to control your diet in Mexico than in the US.

But the Most Important Thing Is...

Here in Mexico, you can really enjoy food. You have an abundance of flavors and textures, much more than you would at home.

My advice to you is: Enjoy this fine food, but do it safely and within reason.

But enjoy it.

7

MEDICINE AND HEALTH

Here I try to help you keep your health. Understand your options, and act before you have need. There are many options to study. Mexico's health system is very competent, but it's so convoluted that you need to think about it. Sorry about that. This is not the admirable and humanistic Canadian system, nor the US's free-for-all; this is Mexico's system, and it's good, but it's quite different.

Just like anywhere else, while you live in Mexico you need to pay attention to your health. This involves all sorts of considerations of living right, exercising, eating right, and being prepared for emergencies. I've told you about the foods, but I doubt you can even eat very healthful here, nor that you even want to consider it for the moment, but you need at least to make informed decisions.

If you're just here for quick visits, you're dependent on your own US medical system. I'm so far out of touch that I can't help you there. You just need to know what your system will do for you when you're out of the country. You should know what you do if you have an automobile accident, or what your options are if your teenage daughter gets appendicitis, etc. You get the idea. Check on theses things before you leave.

Of course, how you live is also important. Given that there is a much higher rate of automobile accidents than in either Canada or the US, I would recommend specifically that you do as little driving as possible. Read my chapter on driving, and be eternally vigilant, but it's hard to handle all situations and some accidents do happen.

Medicine in Mexico

Mexico has an interesting mixture of public (socialized) medicine and private medicine. In theory, almost everybody in the country is somehow protected by Social Security, ISSSTE, or the SSA. In theory the *Instituto Mexicano del Seguro Social (IMSS)* system, normally called the Social Security system, covers the private sector (companies of all kinds, that are required to belong). The *ISSSTE* system (*Instituto de Seguridad y Servicios Sociales de los Trabajadores del Estado*) covers the public sector (government or government supported). There is a system administered by the *Secretaria de Salud y Asistencia (SSA)* which includes those persons not covered by the other two.

All three offer medical services at all levels. Social Security and ISSSTE also handle retirement and pension systems, as well as things like housing loans. There is now a tendency to privatize the pension systems to enforce fiscal responsibility (The US isn't the only country with retirement benefit problems).

The three systems work pretty well. A poor person can get primary care in clinics, though the time involved in waiting for services is long. And all members can get all the advanced services that are necessary.

And it needs to be said: There are physicians of all levels in the two systems, including the most sophisticated and highly trained specialists in the country, as good as any in the world. Still, since Mexican students enter medical school after high school (unlike the US, where they enter medical school after completing or nearly completing an undergraduate college course), Mexican doctors usually have less training than US doctors.

In practice, poor persons can use these systems for all their needs, but a person with more resources will tend to avoid the primary services. For all small things, a person that can will skip the lines and go to the private offices of physicians; these can even be the same physicians since most have both public and private practices. For intermediate things, some will go public, others will go private. For the very large things, most people will endure the lines and use the public system, unless they have private major medical insurance, which is what I recommend for you.

A particular decision will also depend on where a person lives. One tends to trust the public systems more in the largest places, as, for example, in Mexico City, where the Social Security facilities are superb. In smaller cities and towns, one trusts the public facilities less.

There are also health insurance policies available, such as major medical policies. These mostly liberate a person from heavy dependence on the public systems. They aren't as expensive as in the U.S. They tend to promote the use of the several excellent private hospitals. Still, the policies don't handle emergencies well (unless you happen to carry about $us 1000 cash with you as a deposit) and you never know just what they will cover. Even in an emergency, you have to get advance permission for treatment. In my experience, regardless of your policy, you will probably have to fight to get the insurance company to pay what it should pay. Read the fine print of your policy, and plan on having a lawyer on your side.

The overall Mexican system is admirable. In general, it tends to give fair support to almost everybody, including most poor campesinos in isolated areas. It has many defects, but overall it is quite sound.

Care Options for Foreigners

If you work in Mexico, your company will probably have coverage available by the Social Security system. You can learn first hand how it works.

Still, for ordinary health care, most foreigners with a bit of money don't use any special system. (And if you don't have a bit of money, Mexico doesn't want you here!) They just go to a doctor when they need to, and pay from their own pocket. Most physicians' charges are still low enough for that. And since there is an excess of physicians, especially in the large cities, that's not likely to change, at least for ordinary Mexicans. Of course, there are physicians that specialize in Gringos, and they charge more.

I'm not going to tell you how to choose your physician for day-to-day care. If you know other Americans, they can help you, and the American Embassy maintains a list of physicians. You can always consult the better hospitals in your area to find out which of their physicians maintain private offices. (Most do, of course.)

For major medical problems you should have some kind of private insurance. There are several major medical care options being offered. Just don't wait. Make sure you sign up *before* you have need.

Mexican Public Health Systems

By law, every hospital must give emergency care as needed without previous payment. This means that if you have an emergency, member or not, you will be treated, at least in a basic way.

As soon as you are stable, the hospital *will* collect for the care given. That's when you need your medical insurance. If you don't have any, you will still be required to pay. People lose cars and houses and other things if they don't pay their medical bills. You are familiar with the system!

Even if you are a member of one of the public systems, the rule of thumb is that none of them is good for small things. You have eternal lines and peculiar procedures for almost any ordinary illness or infirmity. Poor people have no option, but for these things your best bet is to pay to see a physician in his ordinary unofficial practice.

The same rule states that for the big things, major surgery, cancer treatments, and the like, both systems are fine. Both tend to have the best physicians in the country, excellent hospitals, and state-of-the-art equipment. It's socialized medicine, and it's excellent. If you don't speak Spanish you should realize that you won't find much English spoken in these systems.

But probably most foreigners will depend on separate major medical insurance policies to handle these major problems in private hospitals.

Just Watch Your Health

With exception of automobile accidents, if you take care of yourself your risks in Mexico won't be any greater than they are at home. There may even be fewer risks than at home!

So take my advice. Drive less, or don't drive at all. Eat as healthy as you can. Get exercise. And prevent problems when you can.

That's almost the same advice you'd get at home.

But it's still good.

8

YOU CAN'T EVEN CONCEIVE OF AN HONEST COP!

"Can't anything be done, sir?" "That's up to you, sir." This is a conversation you will eventually have with a person in a police uniform. But don't despair! We show how to live through it all. You will also come to realize that these "enforcers of the law" have gall that Hannibal would have admired.

When I was a boy I used to talk with my grandfather about the old days in Chicago, around the turn of the last century. He was an immigrant, among many, and in those days scratching to make a living and support his young family.

I really had a hard time believing some of his stories. Many had to do with police in his neighborhood that were on the take, police openly on the side of criminals, things like that. But I had been raised to *trust* the police and I had heard nothing of things like that.

It turns out that he was right and I was right. By the time I was a boy Chicago had pretty well cleaned up its act. Later I learned that Chicago wasn't the only place with that kind of problems, but most had been mostly successful in cleaning up their police departments. Not completely, of course; there are always a few weak and bad elements everywhere, but it's no longer an overwhelming problem. And to tell the truth, the quantities of money involved in the drug traffic can probably corrupt any body of policemen in any part of the world.

And then I came to know Mexico.

You need to understand that I feel so bad about this chapter I have to explain. This is the one chapter I didn't want to write. Mexico is one fine place to live. But the police are a gigantic stain on the fabric of the Mexican society. And although there are gigantic reforms underway, nobody is very optimistic about them over the short haul.

That is not to say that all police are crooked. Mexicans of my age remember when police were presumed to be honest, and they remember when all that changed. There are now, and there always have been honest police. In addition, the top officials in charge of the police are quickly changing things for the better. Young people with a new vision are entering police departments all over the country. I have no doubts about a final success simply because the public is demanding it with a force that cannot be stopped.

Still, the process will take many years. If you're going to live here, you'd best understand the situation, or at least you'd better understand how it's different here than in the US.

Trusting Police

The problem of police is the most vexing of problems, a tremendous shadow over an American's view of Mexico. With reason, most modern Americans tend to trust police, at least within limits: we wouldn't just leave a thousand dollars cash lying around in a police station. But then, we wouldn't leave them around the house, either. After all, people are people, and temptations affect us all.

But Mexicans have no reason to trust police for any reason. Ask somebody how many times he's been robbed. He or she will probably recount none or just a few times. But ask how many times he has been "bitten" (*mordido*) by the police, it's sure to be many times.

Myself, I've never been personally assaulted while walking on the street, though many of my relatives have been held up a few times. But we have *all* been held up by the police. For people who spend a lot of time driving, it's probably on the average a monthly or more frequent occurrence. And for other kinds of crimes, I'm sorry to say that the first suspects are usually police and former police and security guards.

That is to say, organized crime is a problem, and at first glance, just eliminating the police would eliminate the problem. Except, of course, that there are legitimate things for the police to do. And in Mexico they do them too!

But look at the problem. A large fraction of holdups are made by *uniformed* police without badges. Many of the rest are made by people in uniform, fake police that are seen everywhere. Many, maybe even most, of the rest are made by former police, that don't know any way of making a living than being on one side or the other of the game of crime. Maybe the rest are crooks without police training, although some of these are former soldiers.

Things are Changing

At this writing, things are being done. The most respected rights officials in the country have been appointed chiefs of the police system. They are actively working at the problem.

But it takes more than the dramatic rectitude of the top boss to deter a Mexico City cop. The same week that I saw a dramatic public diagnosis of the problems, praised by all the political parties and criticized by none, I saw an informal interview of a cop on the beat, in which he explained that even though his wage was low, he was obliged to pass his quota to his superior, and his quota was 500 pesos ($us 60) per day.

Things are changing. But they haven't changed much yet. Frankly, the system penetrates so deeply that hardly anybody believes they will change in the near future, despite all the actions and rhetoric.

9

WHY DON'T THEY DO SOMETHING ABOUT THE POLICE?

Well, it's not for not wanting or trying. But I doubt if there is any practical way to do it quickly. The tradition is so strong and so deep that I don't see any easy way out, and I don't know anyone that does. Let me tell you why.

Why not just clean up the police system? You just fire, or jail, the dishonest cops, and that's that.

Well, it's just not that easy. Cleaning up Tammany Hall, or Los Angeles Police racism, or Chicago police would be easy by comparison. The tradition is very deep, it's been going on a very long time, and most people wouldn't even know how to behave towards them if the cops tended to be honest.

What a Young Man Expects

Consider this. I know of an institute that had always survived without organized security guards. Sometimes there would be a guard for handling money, like salaries in cash, but generally they didn't have guards even for such things.

One day the decision was made to protect equipment from theft, and a professional guard service was hired, with around-the-clock guards at the entrance of the institute, in the buildings, in the parking lot, and other places.

Then it was noticed that things started disappearing from the refrigerators in some offices. The theft was traced to the guards. That is to say, theft, or at least petty theft, was *increased* by having guards.

What does that mean? Simple. The mentality of police and uniformed men of all kinds is that they are to enforce the law, but that they are above the law.

You doubt this? Just try to drive the way you see patrol cars driven. They drive as though they are above the law. They know. Sorry to say, they are.

And when you start with that kind of premise, the Mexican system of traffic cops, security agencies and all the rest comes into focus. The expectation of a kid going into the cop business is that he is above the law.

But in spite of this cultural base, things are changing.

The General Public Cooperates

It's very easy to say it's the public's fault for bribing the cops. It's certainly true to a certain extent, but as a member of the public, I can answer that. I can answer that as a resident of another state, I have no options when faced by a hungry patrolman on Zaragoza Avenue, a main entrance to Mexico City. The system has been devised with a view towards detaining persons with out-of-town license plates.

With out-of-town license plates, I will never just be given a ticket and left to drive off and pay the fine later. I will be detained hours or perhaps a day or more if I don't pay the patrolman. I will have to drive to one of the local police offices and face the local authorities, all *without the presence of the person who detained me* and without having been able to see the charges made against me. The burden is on me, and innocent or guilty, I will have to pay. Even worse, even if I were guilty of something when I was stopped, that's probably not what will be on the ticket.

The patrolman loses money if he leaves the battlefield. His loss is such that he will never leave if he can avoid it. Some theoretical affection for justice just can't compete with the money that can be earned and that probably *he must earn if he is to keep his job*. There is just no way I will ever be able to confront the man in front of an impartial third party. Unfortunately, in the experience of most, there is no impartial third party involved in any case since the money extorted on the route is spread through the office personnel, so all have a vested interest in continuing the system.

Ask any taxi driver. If he doesn't pay on the spot, his ticket will include many offenses not committed, always including disrespect to an official of the law. He has no rebuttal.

Can't Anything be Done?

Of course, lots can be done. Some important things are even being done.

A remarkable example is the current tow-away policy, which is certainly extremely enlightened and eliminates abuses which were frequent before. In all cases, in Mexico City, if you arrive before your car is towed away, you may take a ticket and keep your car. This partially eliminates the traditional police policy of impounding cars to strip them.

At the present time, a policeman should wear his badge in plain view, but many don't. They are not obliged to identify themselves, and so they act anonymously. In addition, often they use patrol cars without licenses or other identification. It would not be difficult to cure these defects.

But it's hard to do most of the things that need to be done. As it is, if a person doesn't pay the bribe, he has to go to the local police station, *without the presence of the person who detained him*. It would be easy to require the detaining patrol car to go with him. But, of course, this would reduce the number of patrols on active duty. But even worse, from the point of the view of the patrols, it would cut their time in the lucrative bribe business. While in the station they could not be collecting bribes.

I have no doubt that the president of the country wants to reform the system. It's also evident that the fine men from outside the system who have been assigned to head the police want that, and it's evident that the public wants it. But I doubt that the president, or anyone else, is willing to pay the very high price required to do it quickly. Eventually it will be done.

One of the chief weapons of a dishonest patrolman is the size of the fine. The regulation book of most patrolmen is only used to show the cost of a fine if we don't pay bribes. Despite our principles, many of us feel it necessary (or at least convenient) to pay a lesser bribe than a large fine. Lower legal fines would defuse this problem. But the tendency has been to raise fines. As an example, it's evident that lives are saved by raising the fines to high levels for not using seat belts; but that also supports corruption.

There are many other alternatives. Mexican ingenuity could find a way, but it will be difficult.

The Dimension of the Problem

By any accounting, the problem is gigantic. There have been several estimations which I won't repeat, but you should just reflect on the number of traffic police in a city the size of Mexico City. All those mtorists, taxis and busses represent a source of money that just can't be overlooked by any politician on the make.

The problem was at its worst during the administration of the police chief named Durazo. If you're interested in such things, look for the book, "*Lo Negro del Negro Durazo*," by José González (Publishing house: Posada, Mexico City, 1983, LC JL1299.D576 C64). I'm sorry to say it's not available in English.

We need to recognize that the problem cannot be limited to the cop on the beat. The political reality is that with that kind of money involved, it involves more people. It certainly involves the level of supervisors, who, after all, graduated from the street and are well acquainted with the system. Do you think they would allow the men on the street to extract these quantities of money without insisting on taking their share?

And if they take their share, do you think *their* supervisors won't insist on their share? After all, they also understand the system. They graduated from the street, most of them.

And do you think that any of them will really be in favor of reform?

Next, you need to recognize that it is not simply a problem of extortion of drivers. It is combined with law enforcement in a subtle way, which actually results in enforcing the law but also extortion of the city. For example, if you accidently drive into Mexico City on a day forbidden because of your license plate number, you will be shown the book showing the fine and given the option of paying the bribe or accepting a ticket. So when you pay the cop, you are actually cheating the city of its revenue. You and the cop are "benefitted" in some way, but the city loses its revenue.

So What to Do?

Police in other countries are not morally superior to Mexican police. It's just that they work under different rules. If Mexican police know they will lose their jobs if they shake people down, most, but not all, will stop shaking people down. They will be in a serious personal dilemma because they are accustomed to a higher standard of living than their salaries can stand, but still, they will generally opt for keeping their jobs and staying out of jail. And nobody really cares if they choose to leave their jobs because there are plenty that would die to get their jobs even without the extra income from the bribes. Getting a job in this country is not easy.

After making it known that you were going to crack down, you could crack down. You note that from then on, no cop would be able to trust his partner, nor any other cop, nor his supervisor, or even any other uniformed person. You have made it known, so there are no excuses. Then you *really* crack down.

There is certainly no difficulty in having cops shake you down. It used to happen to me all the time. Driving into Mexico City with out-of-state license plates is normally enough to do it. If, like me, you look like easy prey, it will happen to you. Pay each man off and secretly take a picture of him at the time. At the end of the day, prepare your dossier, and go after them.

If you are not just stopped spontaneously, as I normally am, give them an excuse to bug you. Drive with a car on a forbidden day. You will be stopped. Do it in various parts of the city and see how many times you are actually ticketed, and how many times you are able to pay instead. After the first time you have to change your license plate because the communication system between patrol cars is very efficient; everybody will notice if you try to get caught a second time with the same plates, and your sting will be over.

Run a taxi for a while, and give the patrol cars a minor reason to stop you. Then refuse to pay your bribe. Then when you go to pay your fine, see what the ticket says you did. Normally the patrolman is so irritated over his failure to collect that he will invent several new charges, always including disrespect for an officer. Do it with several different taxis. At night, compile your dossier.

I have to admit that authorities have recently developed a system that even I hadn't considered. For the moment they've forbidden all male traffic cops from giving tickets. Only female agents are allowed to, on the theory that the women are less liable to accept bribes. Since there are extremely few women among the agents, it is a very interesting experiment, but first results are not encouraging. Let's hope it works. It does show that the authorities are trying to control the situation.

What about Better Salaries?

There's no doubt that better salaries are needed for all varieties of policemen. Some are paid so little that they can't actually survive on them. But that is also true of other type of government employees. And at any level of wage, there are many more qualified applicants than jobs.

Boost salaries? Of course, but in the context of bettering salaries for all of the really low-paid government employees.

That said, there is little point to just raising salaries for police. The people applying to be police (or anything else, for that matter) are implicitly accepting a kind of job that is remunerated in a certain way. If the remuneration is higher (or lower, for that matter), different people will apply. Raising salaries and training requirements will, in most cases, only be useful for attracting a different kind of person.

For the patrolmen of Zaragoza, you need to recognize that you will never raise salaries to the point that they will be tempted to work honestly. The government just can't pay that kind of salaries for patrolling the streets. Again, the people who accept patrol jobs without the possibility of shakedowns will not be the current generation of patrolmen. Who knows if they expected to live so high when they applied; but after that experience, they would certainly not accept lower-paying jobs unless there were no options for gathering money on the side.

10

POLITICS IS NOT A DIRTY WORD

But it's not very clean, either. Politics is the favorite national sport of Mexico, closely followed, of course, by soccer. Every daily newspaper has endless interpretations of the meaning of this or that development within one or another party, or level of government, or other country's government, or even the United Nations. There are even daily newspapers specializing in politics.

I'm not a person to condemn politics. It's obviously the art of doing the possible with what's at hand. That is to say, it is expedient, and it is what you need to get things done. Without politics nothing in government would ever get done. Indeed, little would be done at all, even outside government, since there is always someone opposed to doing whatever somebody else wants done.

But whereas politics is considered a necessary evil in the US, in Mexico it's something that interests almost everybody.

Now let me give you a very simplified practical introduction to politics in Mexico. I'll leave the learned discussions of political theory to the academics, but you need to know where you are and just how things work. And you need to cope with the strange things you'll see that are alleged to be the normal operation of government. As I say, this is very simplified. With time you'll understand much more.

Take NAFTA as an Example

There's an informed consensus in Mexico, as well as in the US and Canada, that this North American Free Trade Agreement is for the good of all three nations, both in the short and in the long term. There are obviously politicians who vote against it, but a large number say, privately, that they recognize that it's necessary but that on the short haul they can't go against the wishes of their particular electorates. In particular, the trade unions of the US don't like the possibility of what appears to them to be the export of lower level jobs of their members, though serious studies indicate that this is more than compensated by greater increase of higher level jobs, which is where the children of their clients are headed.

It's even more important for Mexico than for the US and Canada. There are disadvantages, such as vulnerability to international monetary currents, such as the one that caused the devaluation of 1994. But on the long haul, it's obviously necessary if Mexico is to develop enough simply to employ its growing population and perhaps even to increase its average *per capita* income, which is even more difficult.

But in all three countries, actually being able to sign the treaty was an act of creative politics. I won't go through the gyrations in the US, which were fascinating, but the problems in Mexico are quite different.

Given the explicit anti-American bias of the leftist parties, formerly the active admirers of the Soviet Union and even, in many cases, of admirers of Maoist China, many felt (and still feel!) that even signing a treaty with the US was an act of dealing with the Devil himself. So even the *signing of any pact* involved the political calculation of the power of the opposition.

Mexico is Centralized

The Mexican view of government is vitally different from the US. You need to understand this, because many misconceptions can cause problems if you don't.

Most colonizers of what are now the US and Canada went with the idea of staying. Many of the very first were escaping religious persecution. Others were escaping grinding poverty, or even prison. Their reasons for migrating were varied, but the common idea among them all was that they were going to stay.

By and large, when they could they took their families. They understood the concept of self-government and they expected to exercise it in the new land. (It's not necessary to note that the royalty governing England and other countries at the time was hardly open to such ideas.)

But the colonizers of Mexico came from a different time, with a different kind of home government in back of them, and their motives were different. They came alone, probably for some adventure, but to get money and go back to Spain and live as grandees.

There wasn't even the idea of democracy in their times, except perhaps as a historical idea of Rome. Spain was an absolute monarchy, and all power was wielded in the name of the crown. All power was *all power*, and that included the religious as well as temporal power. The authority to govern was absolute.

Through the years things evolved a bit, but after the Mexican national revolution against Spain, power was centralized, this time in Mexico City. Though the country has a nominal federal system, the United States of Mexico, inspired by the US federal system, in practice (and certainly, also, by necessity in the early years) all power was vested in the central government.

It still is, although now not so much for necessity. There are many honest initiatives towards decentralization of power, and some changes have been made, but the system is still *controlled* by the central government. The central government controls taxation at all levels, and that's just one symptom of the implicit centralism in the country. For signing the NAFTA treaty in the US, there was need of legislative approval; that is to say, persons directly responsible to the citizens had to approve the treaty. In Mexico, it was up to the president; if the legislature was required to approve, it was a sure thing, in those days, at least.

There are strong changes afoot in Mexico. Now it wouldn't be automatic.

The Citizen's View

What's important for you to know is the view of the ordinary citizen towards government. If not, when you talk about *government* you'll be talking about different things even though you use the same words.

Let's take the fairly recent US embargo against Mexican tuna, that in theory has ended. We know that American tuna fishermen were in favor of the embargo and exerted their political power; that's to be expected (but deplored). But the real power came from conservationist groups. Dolphins were being killed by the technology then in use, and according to conservationist groups, that's not fair. Dolphins are intelligent creatures, and there's even hope that people will eventually be able to communicate with them.

But to most Mexicans, the conservationist argument didn't (and still doesn't) make sense. To their way of thinking, the *government* could just declare the embargo, or undeclare it. Anti-American forces in Mexico didn't help matters, since their idea is to sour relations between the countries. But the fact that the US government was responding to the conservationist lobbies just couldn't be understood.

That is to say, government to Mexicans has always been almost a monolithic structure that makes decisions without input of citizens. If the president decides, well, that's it. In practice, this is no longer quite true, but still, it's the average Mexican's understanding of government. Quite literally, it's the only kind of government he's ever seen or been associated with.

What about the rights of a government worker? That the US government could even respond to a Civil Service is equally incomprehensible to

Mexicans. There is no civil service in Mexico, at least not as an autonomous organization that gives rights to employees. There are only unions. It's the government that hires and fires and sets responsibilities. That's why government employee unions are strong in Mexico. However, as a practical matter, most of the unions respond to the government instead of their members, and as a result, independent unions are beginning to gain force. Like I say, the country is changing rapidly.

Powerful Families

Like Mexico, the US has always had its powerful families. They wield economic power in the US, but they wield economic *and* political power in Mexico. That's the way it was, but things are changing.

In the colonial days in Mexico, there was no pretense of self government. In theory the Crown ruled; in practice, the powerful ruled both in government and economic power. After the separation from Spain as result of their War of Independence, the power elite was in charge. It wasn't until 1910, when the Mexican Revolution happened, that there was a pretense of self government in Mexico for ordinary people. And it's been an uphill battle since then to change from a one–party government to a more pluralistic system.

As with most revolutions, one oligarchy succeeded the older one. The revolutionary language belied the real facts. The new rulers of Mexico tended to be just a few powerful families, but not necessarily the same ones as before. Still, the seeds of democracy were sown, and that started an irreversible process.

The Law

Mexicans especially want their country to be ruled by law. But that's not going to be easy. Tradition has it that many people are above the law. The term in Mexico is *impunity*. For years, now, there have been politicians and rich persons who have enjoyed *impunity* for anything they did.

But Mexicans have lost their patience. They are honestly tired of it, and the new generation of politicians is recognizing that. Little by little the opportunities of politicians to loot and corrupt are being reduced. But this is a big step, and it takes time.

I should add that hardly anybody believes in justice by the courts. If you are involved in an affair with the police, you have to bribe, openly, to get your matter dealt with. Everyone (including myself) knows of persons who have been mistreated by the courts, just because the opponent had money or friendship with the authorities. Since all judicial matters are handled by single points of contact or very few such points, there is ample opportunity for *buying justice*. But of course, bought justice is no justice at all. With all its defects, most people recognize that a jury system is superior, if only because it's hard to bribe all members of a jury, but there's essentially no chance at all of instituting a jury system in Mexico.

Recent Developments

If there are Mexicans reading this book, I beg their forgiveness for the following simplifications. I'm not giving a profound analysis of current politics in Mexico. I'm just trying to give some background information that will help Americans understand the current political environment. What I say will be full of oversimplifications, but it should serve as a decent starting point for Gringos trying to understand Mexico.

As I write this, things are changing fast in Mexico. For years there has been one official party, the PRI (Revolutionary Institutional Party) that has governed. There's been an ever changing field of opposition parties, which have never had much more than a vocal existence; that is to say, they complained, and they had some influence because of their voice, but they never really participated in practical matters of government.

The PRI tended to be centrist by definition, but it was in essence an umbrella which could host a wide divergence of political tendencies. Within the PRI you had rightist groups, you had leftist groups, and there was a large central core.

The PAN (National Action Party) has been home to people with more rightist views for many years. Over the years it has developed into a powerful party with a fairly stable set of principles. Industrialists and some of the wealthier tended to be formal members, but there was a large body of people who were in favor of the principles of the party. To some extent, there was an overlap with the PRI, which also had a large right wing inside the party.

There has always been a large and floating set of leftist parties, including Trotskyist, Maoist, and more with modern Communist or Socialist tendencies. There have also been *alliance or unity parties* that grouped members of these so that their votes wouldn't fragment the ballot.

But only recently, the PRD (Party of the Democratic Revolution) has come to enjoy fairly wide support of large fractions of members of the older leftist parties. The PRD is adapted to the modern world without the presence of the Soviet Union or Maoist China, and, indeed, seems to be fairly well adapted to the modern capitalist regime, but with more protection of the workers. It's interesting to note that in general, the directors and the founders of this party come specifically from a group within the PRI called the *Democratic Current*.

As I write this, both the PAN and the PRD have won sufficient elections to challenge the PRI: the PRI monopoly of government is now over. Both PAN and PRD have won sufficient governorships and mayorships to challenge the PRI.

Throw them Out!

It has almost always been possible for the electorate to *throw the bastards out* in the US when it disliked the government as it developed. It had never been possible in Mexico.

For the first time, it is now happening in Mexico. Such is the new world of Mexico. In the most recent elections in Mexico, PAN and PRD have been able to throw the PRI out. It's a new world, a healthier world

Lest you Misunderstand

I am trying to help you understand the Mexican environment and, in this chapter, the Mexican government, political, and legal system. Frankly, I am oversimplifying. I know of no other way to introduce you to this subject.

Take note that I am not criticizing! The Mexican government in modern times has worked, and has granted stability and continuity to Mexico. With exception of very few countries in Latin America, only in Mexico has there been sufficient continuity for the sustained development of the country. You shouldn't underestimate stability for the progress of a country.

Mexico's government has served it well, judging from the rest of Latin America. Still, it's now in a new transition, towards a multi-party system. Let's trust it will work. I, personally, am confident it will develop into a healthy system with the continuity the country needs.

How All This Affects a Mexican's Views of the US

What I've been saying is that for a Mexican, *government* is a relatively unambiguous thing. If the president makes his wants known, that is policy, and *government* does it if it can be done.

So when something happens in the US, it seems to a Mexican to be a monolithic thing. To change something, you just need for the US government to change. Fat chance! Still, that's the way it's always been in Mexico.

As most advanced governments, Mexico has abolished the death penalty, as well it should. The US has not abolished the death penalty. I won't say that the president of the US couldn't wield power and perhaps influence the Senate and the House of Representatives, but the probability of his being able to abolish the death penalty is rather low. It's considered a state matter rather than a federal matter, and frankly, the public is in favor of the death penalty in general. That's why the states have it.

Convince a Mexican that the US government can't abolish the death penalty? That simply goes against common sense. In Mexico, the government did it. So much for common sense, which, unfortunately, depends on local customs and experience. In any case sometimes no kind of sense works with government.

Mexicans, on the other hand, are familiar with the lack of power of the vote. For years, Mexican votes were on a par with Cuban or Russian votes. The only possible negative vote was an abstention.

But things are different now. Stay tuned to see how it turns out.

11

A CHILDISH PLEASURE:
DRIVING IN MEXICO

Driving is fun in Mexico, but it's also dangerous. I think you should avoid driving. But if you do drive, know the risks and protect yourself. There are certainly fewer accidents now than before, but still there are more than you imagine. You think you know the real rules of traffic in Mexico? I doubt it. Read on and see.

What a terrible thing to say! A childish *pleasure, indeed! But so many things are accepted in Mexico that are prohibited in the US or Canada. For example, even as the light is changing from yellow to red, you can drive into an intersection and block traffic on the other street. You shouldn't, of course, but you can! You see it all the time!*

Thinking of driving to Mexico? Good idea. It's a beautiful place. The people are wonderfully hospitable. Your money goes a lot farther than at home. The scenery is varied and magnificent. You have fine hotels of all kinds in all price ranges, and it's fascinating just living in a culture that's truly different from that of the US. I can almost guarantee you'll have a fine time.

But don't take chances by just driving as if you were in the US or Canada. It's no insult to say that Mexicans drive different than Americans. It's just a fact, and they'll tell you that. And if you are not prepared for the differences, you could spoil that lovely vacation.

Thinking of living in Mexico for a while? You need to be even more careful. You'll be facing even more situations you're not prepared for.

Nothing is more terrible than a serious traffic accident in a strange place. Here I hope to peel away some of the misunderstandings most people have so that you can avoid accidents. When you finish this chapter, I trust you won't be as naive as I was when I first drove in Mexico.

A Caveat

Baja California is a different traffic world, one that surprises Mexicans from the rest of the country. In its traffic Baja seems more like the US state of California. In particular, pedestrians usually have priority in most of Baja (but certainly not always).

In this book I'm talking about most of the rest of Mexico, which is quite different. It's my experience that driving is very similar in most areas outside of Baja. What I tell you here should serve for almost all of the country.

The Formal Rules

Actually the formal rules of traffic are mostly the same as in the US. There are differences, but not many. Some are vital, and I'll explain them. I'll also tell you about signs, some of which are not immediately obvious.

Things change fast here. I can only give you my best impression of things as they are right now. You need to find a way of getting up to date. On bringing cars into Mexico and on border affairs, on the US side, check with the American Automobile Association anywhere in the US. In border cities and principal cities of the border states, you can check with the Sanborn's Insurance Agency, which specializes in such things.

Documents

A driver of a Mexican car needs the equivalent of a driver's license, license plates, a document authorizing that the car can be used, proof of payment of the yearly tax on the car, a special sticker with the license number, a certificate that it doesn't contaminate the air, and recently in some places, proof of insurance. In Spanish, you need *licencia de manejar, placas, tarjeta de circulación, paga de tenencia, engomado, verificación de anticontaminación, y prueba de póliza de seguro.* For a tourist, the US or Canadian driver's license will be acceptable. If you become a longer term resident, you'll need to get a Mexican driver's license, but that's not difficult.

If the car has American license plates, you have to bring it in under special conditions as a tourist, and you can get permission to use it for only six months; this could require a cash deposit or a bond equivalent to guarantee that the car leaves when you do. You must keep the importation documents in the car, including proof of insurance policy. But you must not let a Mexican drive it unless you are in the car with him. Otherwise imported cars would be used as substitutes for Mexican cars, and that isn't permitted.

Speeds

First of all, you Americans need to understand *kilometers per hour* instead of *miles per hour.* Mexico uses the metric system, like almost all civilized countries. Get some conversions in mind, considering that 100 kilometers is the same as 62 [62.14] miles. (100 miles is the same as 161 kilometers):

45 km/houris28 miles/hour
60 km/houris37 miles/hour
75 km/houris47 miles/hour
88 km/houris55 miles/hour
100 km/houris62 miles/hour
120 km/houris75 miles/hour

Some highways are marked at 120 km/hour, but you shouldn't go so fast. It's rarely safe. You'll likely hit an unexpected defect in the road, or bicycle, or goat, or even a person, even on the safest limited-access super highways.

Small cities and towns are often marked with unreasonably slow speed limits. I say this because you find no cars going as slowly as the signs require. Apparently the idea is to warn the motorist, as well as to give the traffic cops an easy way to fine (or extract money from) a motorist. Here you should always slow down, but to a reasonable extent, and at least take the sign as a warning.

As a practical matter, you should *always* drive conservatively and defensively in cities or towns. In my city you are liable to find in the street in front of your car, often unexpectedly: kids, playing, pedestrians, street vendors, push carts, dogs and cats, cows, horses and donkeys, bicycles, motor scooters, motorcycles, demonstrations and religious processions, taxis and collective taxis, city buses, intercity busses, all sizes of trucks, some in deplorable state, stalled vehicles of all kinds, and, of course, other passenger cars, in all sizes and states of repair. You need to be able to actively *avoid* collisions, regardless of whose legal fault they might be.

Roads and highways between cities are another problem. There are high speed toll roads, there are marked highways used by most tourist traffic (such as the principal routes from Laredo to Mexico City), there are other highways used mostly by Mexicans, many unmarked, and there are lesser roads. In all cases you are likely to find people or animals on the highway. You have to use your good judgement. You need to drive somewhat differently in all these types of roads.

In all cases, obey the posted speed limits when you can do so safely, even when you see other drivers speeding past you. They may be locals who are friends of the local police patrols, or they may know when and where the patrols are to be found. You won't know any of this, and so you should simply obey the posted limits.

Where highways cross small towns or even tiny one-or two-house villages, slow down, even though others don't even pause. Others have knowledge that you don't. Sometimes these are safe hiding places for patrols. In any case, these are places where kids cross the road, and you don't want to hit anybody.

Signs

Signs are there for everybody's protection, but to an English speaker, not all are obvious.

Alto (a red octagon) or, in a rare case, *para*, means *stop*. Until you understand the informal rules, make sure you come to a complete stop at every one of these, just as you would back home.

Ceder (a yellow triangle pointing down) means *yield*. This one causes trouble. When the sign is visible to both roads, such as the exit lane of a highway and the feeder road, be especially careful. While in the US cars on the feeder road must yield, in Mexico cars on the exit lane must yield to the feeder road! Sometimes you can't tell from the signs which of the two streets should yield.

The letter, E, stands for *estacionar*, which means, park. So, E with a line through it, means *no parking*, and E without a line through it means parking is allowed, often limited by the time specified on the sign.

Another important one is this. Right turns on a red light are not automatically permitted in most of Mexico, though the tendency is now to allow it. An arrow smoothly bent to the right indicates that a right turn, with care, *is* allowed at this particular stop light. Be careful with your reflex to turn on a red; it can get you in trouble.

There are lots of other signs, which Mexican tourist maps and the AAA and Sanborn's will explain. *Topes*, for example, stand for speed bumps (but most are unannounced).

In the US, a curb painted yellow almost always means that you can't park there. In Mexico a yellow curb is completely ambiguous. You never know if it means anything. In my experience, normally it's just decoration.

Traffic lights are almost the same as in the US and Canada, but to tell the truth, they are more civilized! Many traffic lights blink a while before changing. This gives you a nice warning. I wish American traffic lights would do the same.

Still, there are deficiencies. Hardly any traffic lights are traffic activated. You can unnecessarily wait a long time without opposing traffic.

And some are downright uncivilized: you can sometimes find traffic lights in the middle of a block, supposedly for pedestrian crossings. Their only function is to give traffic cops on the take an excuse to ticket you when you fail to come to a complete and absolute stop.

You are most liable to find non-standard lights and signs in small cities and towns. Some of these are confusing. An example are special warning lights. Whereas you must always stop for a red light in the US and Canada, what do you do when you find a flashing red alternating with a flashing yellow light? Well, nobody really knows, but normally (but not always) it means you should just be careful, but that you don't have to come to a full stop.

Some are badly interpreted. For example, many traffic patrolmen assume that if there is, say, a left green arrow, you can only turn left when it's green. That is to say, when you see a standard green light, you can't turn left if there's a left arrow that is *not* on. But of course, unless you're familiar with the intersection, you won't know if there's a left green arrow that's off.

In any case, you will find that the signs and the road markings appear to be made by people who don't drive. In many cases they are completely unrealistic, and often out of your line of sight. (Look up!) That's a problem you must live with. You will find traffic lanes which sometimes just disappear or which are at best discontinuous. You'll find *OK for passing* signs on hills or curves where there's no visibility of oncoming traffic, and many other such aberrations.

There are many illogical and self-contradictory signs. Typical is a no left turn sign combined with an arrow painted on the street indicating a left turn. Also typical is a stop sign on the wrong side of a one-way street that intersects a through street. Often you can't even tell which is the through street from the signs.

It's no wonder that the driving public takes only a passing interest in signs.

Ordinary Rules of Conduct

I can't get into detail here, but the formal rules of courtesy and conduct on the road are about the same as in the US and Canada. You really can't go wrong driving in a courteous way according to the rules you already know. You certainly shouldn't go into an intersection just before the light changes and block the other street, even though others do it.

The Real Rules

Those are the formal rules and signs, most of which are easy to understand. But in practice, Mexicans interpret them differently.

Pedestrian Priority

In theory, pedestrians have about the same priority here as in the US. In fact, pedestrians are allowed almost no priority under any circumstances, though most cars will try at the very last minute to avoid hitting a person.

You must allow pedestrians their priority. But you must not expect other vehicles to do the same. If you are a pedestrian, be very careful.

Patrol Cars

First of all, you may think that police cars are driven in a way that gives a good example, at least, that is, when they are not rushing in special emergencies. It is that way in much of the US, although I can remember when it wasn't.

But by my experience, it's never that way in Mexico. Almost always, Mexican patrol cars are a bad example. Because of the peculiar Mexican police tradition, most patrol cars are driven as if they are above the law (as, unfortunately, they are.) They often don't stop at stop signs or stop lights, they go the wrong way on one-way streets, they speed and use their lights and siren when they shouldn't, and in general they do things that everyone would like to do but shouldn't.

Just yesterday I saw a patrol car enter an intersection of five streets with streetlights functioning, without even using its emergency lights. It made a complete U turn in the middle, of course blocking all the streets. It was obviously the easiest way to make a complete U-turn and return to where it came from. But don't you try that!

Speed

And how about speed? More and more people are conscious of safety and tend to obey speed limits when it is possible. Of course, in many cases one would *cause* accidents if he went the legal speed when everybody else is going much faster. Still, on the highway, most of the motorists between cities tend to obey the speed limits.

I have to say that there is a large minority that doesn't. If you drive at maximum legal speed on a highway, someone is sure to pass you going much, much faster. My earnest advice to you is explicit: stay within the limits.

Stop Signs

I do recommend you come to a full stop at all stop signs. But most Mexicans don't, and certainly, patrol cars never do.

My advice is not absolute. In practice, when they can see that no traffic is coming, most cars will *not* come to a full stop. You need to learn and follow local custom. If you stop in such a case, to Mexicans you are not behaving in a predictable way, and therefore you may *cause* accidents.

Tailgating

Do not tailgate! You know how dangerous that is. Still, you need to understand that hardly anybody in Mexico has taken a driver's education class, so nobody has been formally taught the danger of driving too close to the car in front. In the best of circumstances, brake lights and turn indicators don't always work.

Almost everybody that wants to pass you will come up close behind you and stay until he can pass. This causes many accidents, as you'd expect. Patrol cars do it the same as other cars.

But *don't do it.* Keep your three-second distance (find a point on the road near the car in front of you; you should arrive at that point in three seconds or more). If you can't even keep a two-second difference, *get out of there!* Slow down or get off the road and let everybody pass. Fast driving with too little space between vehicles is just inviting disaster.

The Other Drivers

Good Mexican drivers (and there are lots of them) tend to worry while driving in the US. They see all these competent drivers not preparing for the unexpected. You must drive very defensively in Mexico or you are sure to be hurt. You must be prepared for the unexpected, because in Mexico it will surely happen.

You should certainly use your signal lights. Before turning in either direction, signal with your turn lights. But, don't expect the driver in front of you to do that. Use of signal lights is very sporadic in Mexico, and often the lights mislead rather than help. In general, expect nothing congruent in signaling from bus and truck drivers, who seem to have their own codes. Don't put any trust in signals of taxi drivers, and be at least wary of signals by others.

There are few checks on the condition of cars in Mexico, and many roads are in terrible condition. Don't expect all vehicles to have headlights, tail lights, and stop lights. Many lights are not standard (such as green or amber tail lights). If you are on the road at night, be aware that there may be cars and trucks in bad shape, some without any lights. There will almost certainly be bicycles without lights, and there are often people, animals, carts, and other objects without lights. You may find terrible unmarked holes and other hazards on the road. Cattle may wander onto the road from adjacent pastures.

Driving in Mexico tends to be impulsive and creative. Many drivers don't decide to turn one way or the other until the last minute, and they don't tend to worry about which lane they are in. People will cross left in front of you from the right. It happens all the time.

I have seen taxis with passengers (including myself) back up two blocks facing correctly on a one-way street so they could say they were not going the wrong way on that street. Few taxis would think of driving three blocks when one block on the wrong way of a one-way street would get them to the same place.

On Friday nights and weekends there are many drivers who have been drinking and there are always some who are quite drunk. The message of MADD (Mothers Against Drunk Driving) hasn't been much promoted here, though there are some signs that there will be useful public campaigns against driving after drinking even a little. Designated driver programs are just beginning.

Expect the Unexpected

You must always expect the unexpected. Always.

Once I was going straight, crossing an avenue, when a patrol car turned left in front of me from my right. I was able to avoid a crash by slamming on the brakes, but I almost hit him. The patrol was making a completely illegal turn, and he wasn't in pursuit of anyone, nor were his signal lights on. Still, I doubt that I could have avoided legal responsibility for the accident if I had actually hit him. The patrol is the administrator of justice, and neither he nor his superiors is about to allow him to be charged with responsibility for an accident. The police will escape responsibility if they can. Since they are the arbiters, they normally can.

One-way streets are explicitly one way, sometimes with adequate signs on both ends and at every possible entrance. But there's a certain exhilaration in breaking the law, as every teenager knows. One evening I counted a hundred cars, mostly taxis, going the wrong way, compared with about forty going the legal way on the one-way street in front of my house. You must expect the unexpected! You see, signs reflect a perfect world, but we live in the real, imperfect world. Signs are at best a guide. They certainly cannot control our behavior.

There are good highways, and there are bad highways. Several are so dangerous I refuse to drive on them with my family in the car. If you want to explore one of the most beautiful of these dangerous roads, try the road from Acultzingo (Los Altos de Acultzingo) in the state of Puebla to Fortín de las Flores in the state of Veracruz. The road has such tight curves that trucks have to use the outer lane whether or not it is theirs. Fortunately for those with families and those who don't want the risk, there are ways of bypassing most of these dangerous roads, but certainly not all.

And in many areas there is fog. The fog can be so dense that you can't see ten feet in front, but there will always be traffic. (Acultzingo also has fog!)

Everywhere, people stretch traffic lights. After yellow turns to red, you will still find people crossing. If you don't compensate you can expect trouble. You have to slow down visibly as you stop so the person behind you recognizes you are stopping; jam your brakes and he will surely hit you (and claim it's your fault). And if you are starting up from the cross street, be sure and allow for the late driver stretching his light, crossing in front of you.

Pedestrian priority exists by law, but it never exists in real life. Even in front of the Angel on the most famous and beautiful thoroughfare in Mexico City, in front of the American Embassy, it is worth your life as a pedestrian to cross the road. The only safe way is in the middle of the block, illegally, where you can see what's coming from both sides.

At night, the rules are even more different. Mexicans traveling to the US can't believe that a pedestrian would wait for his pedestrian signal when there are no cars in sight. It just doesn't make sense to them. It makes sense to us because it is a safety reflex to obey the sign that makes us safe, and in addition, it's illegal not to do so.

But not to Mexicans. There is no automatic respect for the law at all. Instead, police and drivers consider the law to be some kind of flexible guide to behavior. Only when a traffic policeman wants to make a point, or write a ticket, will the law be enforced to the letter. But in ordinary driving, nobody feels obliged.

It's worse at night. Then almost anything goes, from running red lights and stop signs to driving at racing speeds through areas that are crowded by day. That's for the sober people. The drunk have even fewer inhibitions at night. If nobody's watching, of course you can do it.

I have stopped at stop signs, when my passengers asked, "Why would you stop here?" When I pointed out the sign, they told me, "But nobody stops here!" That is to say, local custom tends to control, rather than the explicit signs. There are many stop signs that nobody obeys, including, now, myself.

And the Down Side?

As you might guess, the Mexican accident rate is higher than the US. It's not that easy to get traffic statistics for Mexico, but by any count, accidents are much more common. I once compared statistics and found ten to twenty times as many accidents per car in Mexico as in the US. That was years ago, and it's evident that the accident rate is going down everywhere in Mexico. Now there are many more cars but there aren't that many more accidents. There may even be fewer accidents now.

In any case, you should accept that the frequency of accidents is high. Your chances of seeing the remains of an accident are extremely high, and if you don't take precautions, your chances of being in one are very high. You must drive with care, and you should use seat belts at the very least.

You are warned. Driving is fun in Mexico, but you need to know what you are doing and protect yourself.

12

SOME VERY SPECIFIC ADVICE ABOUT DRIVING

I've told you about the problems. Now let me give you some specific advice. I really want you to survive the experience of driving. That's one motive of this book. But you should first understand that it's normally much better to take public transportation, which is, in general, extremely good in all of Mexico. After all, that's how the Mexicans travel. And there are some very important rules for pedestrians, and you must understand how to take taxis.

I hope that by now I don't really need to tell you to check with AAA or Sanborn's before you cross the border driving into Mexico. After you're in Mexico it's too late. I tried, once, but I couldn't get either AAA or Sanborn's things in Mexico City, even though I'm sure they exist somewhere there. It's just something you should do *before* you go to Mexico.

If You are a Pedestrian

When you're walking on the street, as most of us do from time to time, you need to pay attention.

Even though it exists in theory, in practice there is no real priority for pedestrians in Mexico, except in Baja California. At least, I haven't seen any. Drivers hardly even see pedestrians because they know that pedestrians know that roadways are so dangerous. If you step in front of a car the driver may be so astonished that he doesn't even jam on the brakes.

In many places there is no way to cross the street in a protected way. Well thought out pedestrian traffic lights are very rare.

Because of these problems, pedestrians tend to cross streets in any place in the middle of the block.

Traffic police on corners normally worry about the vehicular traffic and they hardly even see the people on foot. They just expect that the pedestrians know how to protect themselves, and they expect them to cross within the changes in movement of cars.

One-way streets are especially dangerous. Many cars go the wrong way. Drivers of bicycles, motorcycles, as well as food or other carts assume that the rules are only applicable to cars and trucks. Of course, patrol cars go the wrong way too..

You should always look both ways, even on one-way streets.

One thing you often can do (and should do in certain places) is cross a street in the middle of the block instead of at the corner. From the middle you can see traffic on both sides, something that often isn't possible from a corner.

Know Where You are Going

Before you go anywhere you should know about differences in laws and customs. Before driving in Mexico you need to get your Mexican insurance in order. All (or almost all) American insurance is completely invalid in Mexico. (Sanborn's insurance has agents only in Guadalajara, Manzanillo, and San Miguel de Allende, so get it at the border before you come in.) You need to know what documentation is necessary to let you take your car (and check for special rules if you think you want to take a camper).

You need to know the basic rules of driving in Mexico, that is, what the laws are and how they differ from ours. And while you're at it, get very detailed trip maps, including times for covering individual stretches of road for your whole trip if you know just where you are going. They are very useful and will probably help more than you may think.

You need to consciously adjust your driving habits to Mexico. That means you must drive more defensively, and you must be prepared to handle the unexpected at all times. *Unexpected* particularly refers to drinking drivers, taxis in a rush, weird turns in front of you, and other inappropriate behavior.

You also need to adjust your driving according to your immediate environment. Driving among trucks on typical inter-city highways requires one set of tactics. Driving on a tourist route requires another.

In all environments, leave yourself room to maneuver. Despite what others do, never tailgate. Follow the three-seconds-behind-the-car-in-front rule if you can. In any case, never be closer than two seconds. And if others persist in tailgating you, slow down or get off the highway until they pass you. Don't take chances.

Young Drivers

In general, I'm not in favor of young Americans driving in Mexico.

Mexico appeals especially to young people in the US and Canada. The fact that it's a free-for-all on the highway, and you can often get away with driving very fast, is an attraction to them. But it can be a fatal attraction.

Let me give a scenario that occurs all too often. I almost fell into this category once when I was much younger, when I first went to Mexico many years ago.

Three young persons want to take an interesting vacation, one that's different, and so they decide to go to Mexico. They have a nice sporty small car they can use. Although they've been driving for five or six years, they've never had an accident in the US. They do tend to drive fast, as young people like to drive, and they hear that in Mexico, there's hardly any speed checks in the country and along the highways between the larger cities (but of course, that's only partially true!).

And to tell the truth, they've hardly seen any accidents in their short driving careers. Serious accidents are now, thankfully, rare in the US. And so they don't think about that part.

And as with all young drivers, they feel immortal behind the wheel.

So they do go. On the highway they drive fast, and they drive close. That's the most exciting way. And that's the way everyone else is driving.

But the unthinkable happens. They are caught between two aggressive drivers on their side and an oncoming problem. They have no escape.

I won't say more, but the ones that survive will be involved in much more dramatic events. Being handled by amateurs in ambulance crews, confronting the highway traffic policemen, the lack of English, the emergency rooms, the hospitals, the financial problems, even exporting the remains of the car. Think of the worst. It happens. And consider the permanent damage, physical and psychological, that's likely to happen to the survivors.

Your Car

First of all, for visitors, I'm not really in favor of the lightest cars. I know they are the prettiest, the sportiest, and they go the fastest. And I know they are the most economical.

But the lighter the car, the more serious the risk to the passengers in even the mildest accident.

So, for Mexican driving, I suggest a bigger and heavier car, even for just a few persons. The size of the car is what most impresses other drivers in city driving; someone will yield to you if you are big, but not if you are small. And the weight will protect you a bit.

I definitely recommend air bags, fastened seat belts, child restraints and door locks, the whole works. Don't take chances.

It may seem ridiculous to have to mention such things, but make sure you have good tires and brakes, your horn and all your signaling and driving lights work, and your vehicle is in good shape. Remember, you're driving where you don't have any reflexes for the rules like you do at home. Make sure you don't have to worry about your own vehicle while you are coping with the outside world.

On the Highway

It's hardly ever necessary to drive from one city to another. The intercity buses come in all prices and degrees of luxury, and by American and Canadian standards, most are quite inexpensive.

Take my advice. Take the first class or luxury buses whenever you want to go from one city to another. You can even enjoy the landscape with safety.

If you do drive, you need to know that there are many different kinds of highways in Mexico. There are the superb high-speed superhighways and toll roads (*autopistas*), excellent highways and superhighways (*carreteras* and *super carreteras*) and ordinary roads between cities. Most are excellent, but some are in poor condition. The majority are congested.

You should also know that Mexican governments of all levels do not accept liability for the condition of the road. If you hit a pothole, or drive off the the road to avoid hitting a person who is dodging a pothole, it's your problem.

Despite the law that explicitly excludes them from high speed highways and most toll roads, you are apt to find bicycles, motorcycles, horses, cattle and pedestrians on all of them. Drive so you can cope when you run across them.

Let's Get Graphic: The Last Time I Drove at Night

I hardly ever drive at night, and neither should you. But for what it's worth, here's how it went last time. I had to start out a half hour after dark. I traveled Mexico City streets, excellent high speed highways, good mountainous highway, and some rough secondary roads, a trip of six hours altogether.

First let me tell you what I didn't see. I didn't see any carnage! On that long a trip I usually see at least one serious accident, but not that night. It was a bright moonlight night, and maybe that helped.

Now let me tell you what I did see, which is what I always see when I drive at night, and what you will also see. First of all, and most annoying, was the bright headlights. I drive in the US, too, and so I can tell you that these were brighter than you see in the US, although there are always exceptions on both sides.

What I saw were headlights mostly aimed higher than in the US. Since there is no inspection of alignment of headlights, lights are aimed wherever a person wants. Your friendly neighborhood car electrician does this for you. *How's that, now? You want them a bit higher? O.K. How's that!*

Since you are at a severe disadvantage if your lights are the way they come on new cars, some people will aim them higher. Otherwise you are defenseless against others that are *really* high.

But as you know, some Mexican drivers are quite aggressive, and even high beams sometimes can't help. Last night, for example, there were many with their lights on high beam that just wouldn't lower them. That makes for some hard seeing. And you know in the best of circumstances, night vision is rather incomplete. Mexicans are aware of the dangers of these roads, and few will sacrifice visibility by lowering their lights for you.

But in addition, I saw: no-eyed, one-eyed, and cross-eyed cars and trucks. There were brilliant halogen headlights, and there were dim regular lights past their prime. There were trucks with white lights on the back (That can really confuse you!), green lights on the back, red lights on the front, in all combinations. *Red* did not mean *rear of vehicle* in many cases. Don't stop thinking when you drive at night: your reflexes may just fail you!

Of course, there were lots of buses and trucks, and relatively few cars. The truck and bus drivers tend to be aggressive in ways we don't expect, and they sometimes seem to be extra considerate, which we also don't expect.

The worst, I think, is the perpetual tailgating with high beams, which, given the height of busses and trucks, aims the lights right into your eyes. They always tailgate before passing, and that gets very dangerous, especially if you lose your nerve.

One truck was remarkable, coming at us from a great distance. He flicked his powerful lights on and off to show that he couldn't or simply wouldn't dim them, but when they were on, they aimed directly into the windshields of oncoming traffic. Even more unexpected was the truck with about a dozen bright *white* lights on the back; apparently they were on a separate switch, because I watched him blink them several times until a car came near, then turn them all off. Of course, he had no other lights on the back, neither red no purple nor other color! I never did understand the meaning of his signals.

On the worst stretch of country road we almost creamed two young teens on their bicycles. No lights or reflectors, of course, and riding on the narrow pavement.

And there was another truck that I can't forget. This was an accident in the making, now or in the near future, and I can't figure out how to tell you to avoid that accident. I had stopped for a red light on a busy thoroughfare. There were two lanes going forward, two lanes going the other way, and crossing them, two double-lane roads. I was on the far right, with nobody on my left.

I was astonished (even I can be astonished in Mexico) when a loaded very large heavy truck simply ran the light. There was no pretending to stretch the light, nor going a bit early on the change of lights. This was just running the red light in the middle of the cycle. Who knows if the driver was drugged or drunk, or if his girlfriend had just left him. He knew that he would survive any crash with a car, and he just didn't care, and so he just ran the light. Luckily there was nobody in the intersection at the moment he ran it at full speed. But on another occasion there will be. That causes really gory accidents.

What can I say? You need to assume somebody is going to do something like that at an intersection, and pay attention. Here you drive scared or you may not survive! Pay more attention than you can even think is reasonable. You'll save yourself, and you'll save others. Do it!

Mexico City

You'll probably want to go to Mexico City. You must know that it's certainly one of the very largest cities in the world, and for a while it was probably *the* largest city. Like other very large cities, it is worth exploring. It doesn't have the ethnic variety of others, but it has almost anything you may be looking for, cultural or commercial.

For the motorist it has an amorphous mass of streets with a very confusing system of names and numbers. Now it also has a roughly rectangular grid of eight-lane one-way streets carved into it, with high speed elevated highways in curved paths through and around it.

Just knowing where you are used to be almost impossible, before they cut out the rectangular grid of streets called the "street axes" (*ejes viales*). Now it's just very hard. Are you prepared for *eight lane streets with fast traffic*? I certainly wasn't. Driving the several high speed highways in Mexico City really releases the adrenaline!

There is one thing you should do before you drive in Mexico City is, of course, prepare yourself. Make sure you have maps and a prepared route. If you don't know your route in advance, you will certainly waste an hour or two. Remember, even if you speak Spanish, the pedestrian you ask for directions probably does not drive, and so he'll give instructions on the basis of what buses or the subway do. That won't help much, especially since there are so many one-way streets and many buses legally go the wrong way on one-way streets in special lanes (something like the "high occupancy vehicle" (HOV) lanes in parts of the US). Excellent maps of the city are available everywhere, especially in the center of the city and in all tourist areas. They are good maps, but remember, they will probably be in Spanish, not in English.

For the likes of most of us, Mexico City is not a place to take lightly behind the wheel. Driving into the city from outside highways is likely to be traumatic because of the sheer volume of vehicles, mostly trucks, buses and vans, virtually all of which are driving at very high, admittedly dangerous, speeds. These entrance routes all end up becoming bottlenecks because of the rapid growth of the city. About all I can say about coming into the city through any of these main highways is: remember all I've been saying, and don't lose your nerve. Don't go faster than you can control, and despite what anybody and everybody else does, don't tailgate nor weave. It's often best to keep to the slower lanes if you can find any.

Fortunately, it is generally easy to get about Mexico City without using your car. Like New York City, it's normally not even appropriate to use your car! The subway (called the *Metro*) is superb and even pretty quiet, and it goes faster than you can expect to go in your car. From all stations there are always taxis, whose cost is generally reasonable. On the *Metro*, as everywhere, watch out for your valuables. Money belts are a good bet.

Mexico City and other big cities always have excellent public transportation and plenty of taxis. You'll get to know the city and people by walking. There are always many buses between cities. First and second class buses are now very safe! Third class buses are something else, but they are still probably safer than your car.

The combination of subway for crossing the city and taxi for shorter hauls can't be beat for convenience and economy: it's cheaper than using your car, less stressful, and faster, too. In any case, you mix with Mexicans and you see more than the traffic in the streets as you do it. If you stay there a while you begin to understand how the Mexicans do it, which is mostly with subway for long hauls, and collective taxis and buses for in-between points.

Wherever you are going to go, you should plan. All good maps have details of streets and subway stations. If something goes wrong, you want to understand where you are so you can figure out how to get back. But in any case, there are always taxis around that can take you where you want to go.

The giant *ejes viales* (traffic axes) cut rectangularly into the city have made driving Mexico City much more reasonable. But these are so large that normal driving intuition fails on them. It's most interesting to watch Mexican drivers at the intersection of two of these monsters. The light changes, and the non-taxi drivers tend to wait until somebody else (usually a taxi or bus) has the nerve to start up. There are always late cars crossing, and there are usually crazy crossers. So the defensive drivers wait until somebody else starts.

You should, too. It's just too dangerous to be the pioneer. Let somebody else move first. If there's no bus or taxi or truck, another ordinary person like you will eventually do it. Let him. It's just too dangerous for you.

There is a complication that traps tourists that drive their own cars. To please certain ecological groups, there are days when certain cars can't drive, called *Hoy no circula*. It's based on the last number of your license plate, and it applies to tourists as well as Mexicans. Some weeks there are two days without driving, depending on the level of contamination of the air. You could be trapped by this system, which, in practice, has encouraged everyone who could afford it to have at least two cars.

I also suggest you consider guided tours. For example, while you are in Mexico City, you really should see the astounding Pyramids of Teotihuacán. They are an hour or two drive out of the city, not accessible by subway and ordinary buses. You could drive, but it's frankly nicer to be able to watch out the window and see what's going on instead of having to concentrate on routes and survival. You should shift gears from the US way of going anywhere on impulse by car and doing a little planning to avoid the use of the car.

Small Cities and Towns

There are certainly many reasons to want to go to small cities and towns. I like to go, just to walk around, visit the church, go to the market, eat a lot of bananas or mangos, participate in the local fairs. Here's where you see what life in Mexico is really all about. Here, if you show that you like being there in a person-to-person way (*You'll find a way!*), you'll find that the Mexicans are lovely people, and that *you* may even be entertainment for them as well as they for you.

If you can find a place to stay, then you can really participate in the rhythms of a town. Of course, it helps to know a bit of Spanish. Almost all places have some kind of hotel arrangement, sometimes just rooms of a local house.

Smaller cities usually have bus service that is fine, and all have taxis. You get to know the city and the people better by walking, but taxis are always available in case you get lost or tired.

But I stray. I must talk about driving instead of just enjoying Mexico. If you *do* drive, you have to drive into town and drive out of town, but that's about it. You want to walk, because that's how you see what's going on. If you have a choice, perhaps you ought to park in the central square, maybe near a police station. If a kid offers to look after your car for you, accept (but tell him not to use the fibre on the windshield). If the car is dirty, accept his offer to wash it for you. That way he won't abandon it. In any case, don't leave objects visible from the outside. Lock baggage out of view in the trunk quite a while before you get to the town.

You could even get to understand the real meaning of time in a small town while you are driving in or out. It's happened to me. On the main street going into or out of town, somebody's likely to stop in the middle of the street to chat with someone, or unload his truck there, and you'll just have to wait. You may think it's a lack of consideration, and of course it is to you, but don't get upset. It's just a tiny thing, because time is worth very little to anybody, and they just can't believe it could be so important to anybody else, even foreigners.

More Precautions

Now let's assume that against all my advice, you've found there are places to go *and you feel you must use your car*. It's always possible of course. If you are new to driving in Mexico, by all means plan your trip carefully before you leave. You certainly don't want to get lost. (I have, many times!)

Drive very defensively. It's not unMexican or antiMexican for me to say that! Many Mexicans do. In fact, that's how they stay alive!

Keep your doors locked and your windows high or closed. Especially in the large cities, there are specialized thieves that look for people in cars that can be easily opened. They will be after you if your car is attractive or if it has visible luggage or things of apparent value. No Mexican that I know drives in Mexico City without locking car doors. Of course, your windows should be closed or rolled up high enough that no skinny arm can reach in and unlock your door.

Plan your trip in advance with a good map. Drive within the speed limits. Drive conservatively. Don't tailgate. Use signal lights, but recognize that others may not use them or what's worse, may use them in a way that misleads.

Always stop at railroad tracks. Most traffic signals don't work reliably. These crossings are axle breakers, so slow down and avoid panic stops.

And always be prepared for the unexpected. Somebody will turn in front of you from the wrong side. Cars will go the wrong way on a one-way street. People do pass on hidden curves, so be prepared to get out of their way if they come towards you.

So What Can We Learn from the Mexican System?

First of all, and most important, we can learn that the US system is not the only one around. In theory there may be international standardization of symbols on traffic signs, but that doesn't mean the real signs are the same nor does it mean that the real rules are the same. Every country is somewhat different, and in Mexico, even every city is a bit different.

That is, ours are not the only way to drive. For the moment ours is admittedly safer, but many of the real rules in Mexico are more reasonable. We should adopt some of them. In particular, we should adopt the blinking of traffic lights before they change.

I think everybody will admit that driving is much more interesting and pleasurable in Mexico. I would like to see it get safer, but interesting will be good even when it's safer!

We should really put much more effort into expecting the unexpected in the US. It's the unexpected that causes problems everywhere.

And if there is one single message I'd like to pass on, it's simply, *Drive defensively!* If it's raining, assume that your brakes or the other driver's brakes won't work—and someday one of them will fail. If the person in front of you weaves just a little, assume he's been he probably has. Expect the unexpected—and someday it will occur.

Finally, in Mexico we see that there are many alternatives to driving your car. It certainly should be possible in the US, too. Many people can't drive safely, and those people should have other ways of getting around. Many don't want to drive in the US, but have no alternative. Mexico shows that it's possible to finance local transportation in many innovative ways, and some of these should also be practical in the US.

A Final Word about Taxis

In most of the world, taxis are very safe. Cabbies tend to be honest and not overcharge, and the vast majority are very protective of their passengers.

Unfortunately, in recent years, taxis in Mexico City have become somewhat dangerous. Some unscrupulous people have taken to using them to assault and rob people. There aren't many bad cabbies in Mexico City, but the few that exist mean you have to take precautions. Sometimes cabs are stolen to be used for assaults.

When you take a taxi that you find touring on the street, you are honestly at the complete mercy of the driver. There is no record of your using that cab, especially since there is no central control of taxis, nor do individual taxi drivers keep records. This has not been a problem until just recently, but I've known people assaulted and robbed by the cabbie, and I've heard of a few fatalities.

You always have the option of calling a "radio taxi" or a "controlled taxi.." In the first, the dispatcher will take your name and there will be a permanent record of your name, your cab, the pickup point, and the discharge point, and the fare will be determined fairly by meter or by previous agreement (but it will be higher than a roaming cab). Until recently, almost nobody made use of radio taxis since it was much more convenient to take a roaming cab, and there was apparently no danger.

Because of recent problems, the government has set up fixed stations where you can take a taxi with confidence and security, just as you find in the airport and bus stations. You aren't registered here the same way as with a radio taxi, but you and the cabby are seen, and that is a protection.

My recommendation now is that in Mexico City you take no taxi where there is no previous and permanent registration. Use radio taxis, or site taxis with registration. Official (controlled) taxis in the airports and the bus stations are also safe. With official taxis you purchase a ticket and give only the ticket to the cabbie. Don't ever pay cash for a taxi ride from an airport or bus station: the cash only guarantees that the cab is not official and the taxi and driver are not known to the local authorities. All these safer taxis are somewhat more expensive than the touring taxis. Still, they aren't much more expensive, and the additional safety is important, especially if you are carrying luggage or a backpack, or if you are tired.

13

TELEVISION (CATCH-AS-CATCH-CAN) WRESTLING

How does the Mexican Everyman see Mexican society? Go to the "catch-as-catch-can" wrestling matches, "lucha libre" in Spanish, and see what the good guys do, what the bad guys do, and how the "authorities" administer the rules. You might do the same in the US, or in any other country, for that matter, if you want to see what the ordinary man knows to be his society's rules. You may not like what you see, but you need to understand. I could also mention cock fights and bullfights, but I won't, even though they are very popular.

I have never seen a cultural analysis of "catch-as-catch-can" wrestling, but I'm positive there are master's theses in sociology, and maybe even doctorates on them. You and I know that this has nothing to do with sports; it's pure showmanship, and indeed, most people who watch also know this. It's certainly not the sport of Greco-Roman wrestling. It just has the *form and the name* of a sport.

But it is a kind of morality play, a fitting subject for commercial showmanship, reminiscent of the Middle Ages, and it's worth your time understanding it. You'll get direct peeks into the Mexican psyche that you won't get anywhere else.

You can watch it on television if you wish, but you'll miss a lot if you don't go to a match in person. It's sort of like the bus ride in the country that I recommend in another part of this book. This is really mingling with the people.

If you say you can't stand to watch such crude spectacles, I'll understand. But you should understand that it is a relatively innocent show. Despite all the posturing, it's not like boxing, where the only real purpose is to inflict enough brain damage to cause the opponent to pass out.

The actors are well-trained athletes, and they are always interesting to watch. And since they are smaller and more flexible than in the US, they do all sorts of things the American wrestlers can't do.

You Are Either Good or Bad

On the advertising poster most of the wrestlers are classified either as *técnicos* (technicians), who are the Good Guys, or *rudos* (rude or rough) who are the Bad Guys. No need to classify the *officials*! They are always bad, always in cahoots with the *rudos*.

The spectators mostly like to identify with the Good Guys. That's easy, because even though they do everything right, they are faced with guys that would do anything to win. That's life!

The Bad Guys take pride in their dirty deeds. They show that it's easier to get ahead by breaking the rules: bit, punch, kick in the groin, whatever it takes. The Mexican saying is, *If you don't play dirty, you don't get ahead!* (*Si no tranzas, no avanzas!*). Crime does pay after all! And though not as many of the audience identify with them, there are certainly lots of fans that do. And you must admit, many of the Bad Buys do what they do with such verve that they deserve your grudging admiration. And in any case, after all, they are only actors.

And then there are the referees, usually at least two of them. They are really bad. They *always* take the side of the Bad Guys, and they even look at times like they are being paid off by them. It's part of the spectacle.

Now, who do you suppose *they* represent? The are the authority figures. You see the police in them, the judges, the governors and the mayors, the bosses and the line bosses, and the like.

So, Just What Are the Rules, Anyway?

Every activity must have rules, and this kind of wrestling certainly does. What are they?

Good Guys should always follow the nominal rules of this kind of wrestling. They shouldn't do things like punching, biting, kicking in the groin, grabbing hair, attacking the referee, having more than one fighter in the ring at a time, things like that. Good Guys usually work alone, one on one. They don't gang up on their opponents in a nasty, forbidden way.

Bad Guys are forgiven any breaking of the rules, except that some rules are unforgivable if you are caught. Worst of all is taking a mask off your opponent, which involves tearing it or unlacing it, usually. You can be disqualified if you kick an opponent in the groin, but usually the referee won't see it if you're a Bad Guy. Few Bad Guys are so bad as to attack the referee openly, and in any case, that might alienate him and cause problems.

Most rules are waived if broken by the Bad Guys. After the first one-on-one sparring, normally the referee permits two or three Bad Guys in the ring, attacking a single Good Guy, but he doesn't allow more than one Good Guy in the ring at a time.

Often the Good Guys win the first round, demonstrating their prowess and their agility with interesting and legal ways of wrestling. But then they lose the second as the Bad Guys and the referees get organized. But sometimes, after a while of taking illegal abuse from the Bad Guys, the Good Guys will just get fed up with being Good Guys and do anything it takes to tackle the Bad Guys. Then even the referee can't control the Good Guys.

Some of the rules in the US are quite different, and Mexican wrestlers have problems with them when they perform in the US. (They also have problems with the size of their opponents. The American wrestlers seem to be giants, now.) In the US you can't throw an opponent over the ropes, you can't dive onto him from the ring when he's on the apron, you can't hit him with chairs…These used to be enforced in the US, even against the Bad Buys, but they occur all the time in Mexico.

It's Also *Tougher* in Mexico

You'll notice right away that wrestling is rougher and tougher in Mexico than in the US. Almost every night of wrestling will cause several wrestlers to bleed, from blows or from biting. That's an accepted risk for these actors.

And all sorts of things are normal that are hardly seen in the US. There's a large part of the action on the apron outside the ring. There are always *mortal dives* from inside of the ring to an opponent outside, making both wrestlers nearly unconscious and tumble to the ground in a hard way. Punches and kicks to the groin aren't seen often in television wrestling, but you see them all the time in local wrestling programs that are not televised. And it's not at all unusual for the Bad Guys to bash the Good Guys with metal folding chairs from the audience. And there are even things like bottle caps scattered on the apron, making things even tougher for the fighters.

So, What's the Message?

The unofficial rules of society are mirrored in all of this. Society really is not on your side. A poor honest guy many has very little chance. Society is really on the side of the Bad Buys. Good Guys are hurt by the rules but not the Bad Guys. Bad Guys work together, but Good Guys go it alone. To get ahead, get away with what you can. In any case, the deck is stacked.

And if you expect help from authorities, well, lots of luck. Authorities have their own agendas, and they might help if you if it's convenient, but don't count on it. That might be in the job description, but not in practice. You're probably on your own.

You may say the message is the same in the US, and I partly agree. US society is not seen to help the poor guy very much. But the wrestling referee seems to have the obligation to do right in the US, but he doesn't in Mexico, and this difference is really important. And there is some physical protection in rules enforcement to protect the players, but there's much less in Mexico; that is to say, you are *really* on your own down here.

So now, Go To It

Wrestling is big in Mexico, bigger than in the US. It's on television, of course, but there are also regular performances in small cities and even in small towns. The smaller the city, the more local talent you'll find (young persons learning the art). But you'll also find there's more acting than on television or in the large cities, simply because it's not worthwhile getting hurt for the smaller revenues in these areas.

Now do as I say. Go out and watch some wrestling. I strongly suggest you visit a local non-televised program. You'll get a better idea of the actors in this way, and you'll even understand the Mexican people better.

Admire the actors. Many of them are superb athletes, and some could even do well performing as gymnasts. In any case, for all of them, it's a specialized ability, giving and taking blows as they do. Some of them perform several times a week, and so you know the damage isn't as serious as it seems.

(This is not to say that there are no dangers. Every so often, even on television, you can see that one of the fighters has fallen badly. This happens mostly in diving from the ring or the ropes onto the apron. Sometimes the actors are very seriously hurt. But this still is not the same as the kind of damage always done in boxing.)

The public is as interesting as the actors themselves. There are often more women than men. You'll even see kids and some adults that believe it's all in earnest. At least they appear to.

The Sad Part of It…

I wouldn't say there isn't a down side to this kind of spectacle. There are certainly several.

Perhaps the worst is that the actors can and do get hurt, sometimes seriously.

The really sad part of it is that the ideas that are behind these performances are, in themselves, self-fulfilling prophecies. If the public really believes them, they will not change.

But the fact is, Mexico is changing extremely fast. The maturity and cultural development of the Mexican public is causing many big changes in society, almost all for the best. NAFTA is partly a result of this new maturity.

But still, the old traditional Mexico, with dishonest self-serving authorities, will always be reflected in these spectacles. To the extent its practices are seen as legitimate by one or another public, this kind of spectacle will inhibit progress.

But This is Especially Important:

I know that in the next chapter I tell you to listen and learn the Spanish language everywhere you go. But there's a problem at wrestling events that you don't have with television.

This is really down and dirty language. It's no language you should ever use. We have it in English in the US, too, and you shouldn't use it there, either. It's the kind of language men may use alone, but everybody you hear in a match seems to be using it.

You may want to understand it, but don't ever use it.

14

You are probably not Embarazada, but maybe you should be Embarrassed!

Studying Spanish is usually not much fun in high school, but you will get a real charge out of learning by immersion in Mexico. You'll have to work at it, but probably you already know more than you think.

I suppose all languages are hard to learn well. But Spanish is certainly one of the easier ones to learn well enough to get by.

Why do I say this? It's just that you need to learn some Spanish. If you're going to spend much time in Mexico, or if you're interested in understanding this country, you need some Spanish. *And if you're not, why are you bothering to read this?*

What Makes Spanish Easy to Learn?

Well, Spanish is *pretty easy* for speakers of English to learn. Let's see why.

First of all, it has fewer important sounds than we have in English (that is to say, fewer *phonemes*.) It really has five vowel letters and only five vowel sounds (a:ah, e:eh, i:ee, o:oh, u:oo). And although its consonants are a little different than the English consonants (not as *hard* or strongly aspirated), they are not very different and they are recognizable. The only new consonants for us are the "*ñ*," which is very easy for us to learn (*en-ye*, of course) and the "ll," equally easy to pronounce as either "eh-ye" or "el-ye" (you can use either one). I should mention that "*ch*" is considered a separate consonant, but that only affects how words are alphabetized, as in dictionaries; it's pronounced the same as in English.

And Spanish is written phonetically. If you see a word written, you know how to pronounce it.

But pity the Mexican who learns English. In English we also have five vowel letters, but we must have about thirteen vowel sounds. Our writing is not phonetic. You just can't pronounce a word if you see it written. You need lots more rules, and they aren't easy rules if you're not born into them.

Spanish also shares many words with English. A large fraction of Spanish words can easily be recognized if you see them written. (*Hearing* them is another matter. You need to train your ears.)

The structure of Spanish is fairly regular and easy, and its grammar is mostly regular. And it doesn't use unfamiliar letters or symbols like Russian or Chinese, so that simplifies things, too.

All in all, you won't have much problem learning enough Spanish to get by in most occasions. And unless you stay in your room all the time, you'll have lots of occasions when you need to understand or be understood.

In any case, you probably already know much more than you think.

Everyday Words and Phrases

You just have to be able to say many small words in Spanish, especially the small courtesy words. It's unreasonable for you not to be able to understand and say all these things at the right time: *hola, buenos días, buenas tardes, buenas noches, bienvenido, adios, sí, no, gracias, muchas gracias, gracias sí, gracias no, sí gracias, no gracias, por favor, hágame el favor, perdón, antes, después, vamos, señor, señora, cuántos años tienes,...*

And I'll bet you understand almost all of these when you see them written: *automobile, autobus, bicicleta, teatro, música, computadora, cine, sonido, tortilla, tamales, presidente, gobernador, lámpara, sal, chile, picante, electricidad, televisión, radio, cable, día, noche, toalla, agua, pintura, color, negro, porche, patio, pasto, ciudad, estado, planta, árbol, flor, maíz.* I'll bet you knew almost all of these words, all closely related to words we use in English or part of common phrases in Spanish.

And I'll bet it wouldn't take you long to add these words to your vocabulary, even though they are different: *comida (food), bebida (drink), cocina (kitchen), mesa (table), pimienta (pepper), silla (chair) cama (bed), sábana (sheet), almohada (pillow), luz (light), foco (light bulb), ropa (clothing), ropa interior (underwear), chamarra (jacket), zapato (shoe), calcetines (socks), medias (ladies' stockings), camisas (shirts), vestido (dress), perro (dog), gato (cat), pollo (chicken), pavo (turkey), servilleta (napkin), puerta (door), ventana (window), blanco (white), rojo (red), verde (green),azul (blue), amarillo (yellow), país (country), arroz (rice), frijol (bean), calabaza (squash), ¿por qué? (why?), porque (because).* It would hardly take you any time at all to add these to your vocabulary since they all refer to things in daily use and you probably already know a few of them.

And Spanish numbers aren't hard at all. You probably know a lot of them now. I'm sure you can figure out the following: *uno, dos, tres, cuatro, cinco, seis, siete, ocho, nueve, diez, once, doce, trece, catorce, quince, dieciseis, diecisiete, diecinueve, veinte, veintiuno, veintidos, veintitres, veinticuatro, veinticinco, veintiseis, veintisiente, veintiocho, veintinueve, treinta, treinta y uno, treinta y dos, treinta y tres, treinta y cuatro, treinta y cinco, treinta y seis, treinta y siete, treinta y ocho, treinta y nueve, cuarenta, cuarenta y uno,..., cincuenta,..., sesenta,..., setenta,..., ochenta,...noventa,...cien, ciento y uno, ciento y dos,...doscientos,...trescientos,..., cuatrocientos,..., quinientos,..., seiscientos,..., setecientos,..., ochocientos,..., novecientos,...mil, mil y uno,...*

In some cases you use *have* in Spanish where you'd use *be (am, is* or *are)* in English. A kid will *have* five years instead of *being* five years old. (*"¿Cuántos años tienes?" "Tengo cinco años."*) You also *have* cold or warmth instead of *being* cold or warm. (*"¡Tengo frío!"*)

Spanish isn't that hard, and you probably know much more than you realize. Still, you need to be able to *hear* the words, which is quite different from reading them, and that requires lots of practice. *That's* the hard part.

And you need to be able to put them together in simple sentences. That's just practice or lessons.

How to Study Spanish

There are now so many ways to study Spanish that you can pick and choose. For many people, classes are best. They almost force you to learn on a given schedule. There are classes for many purposes (travel, conversation, reading,...) and for different types of people(for kids, for travelers, for elders, for businessmen, for women, for college credit,...). It's a rare place in the US where you can't find Spanish classes of several kinds.

If you have a computer with a sound card, there are fine computer-assisted learning programs which include sounds. Some of them even check your own pronunciation. My current personal favorites are the *Transparent Language* programs on CDs (22 Proctor Hill Road, Hollis, NH 03049, tel 603-465-2230, www.transparent.com). The future of voluntary language learning probably lies with computers.

And then there are audio cassettes, video cassettes, and old-fashioned books.

Any and all of these will work if you really want to learn. Classes may even work if you lack self discipline!

You should learn what you can before you come to Mexico, because that makes everything much more interesting and easier. In particular, you should train your ear as much as you can. But also there are plenty of ways to learn once you're in Mexico. You have no excuse for not studying, no matter where you are!

Once you're here, you'll be able to listen to and watch television and read newspapers and magazines; even comic books are great!. Just listening to radio and TV and trying to understand will help a lot, and they will train your ear without your even recognizing it. Newspapers aren't that easy, but they'll help a bit, especially if you try to read the news in Spanish that you have already read in English (there are several English newspapers in Mexico). Comic books are neat: they use only simple common language, even though they may have more slang than you want.

Don't be shy. Practice what you think you know with the people you know. People won't laugh, even when you make mistakes. Basically, people admire your effort to learn the language.

Practicing

I told you that nobody would laugh. That's true. No grown-up will ever laugh at someone's mistakes in learning Spanish, *even when we think he ought to.*

As a matter of fact, that's actually a problem. You need help! You'll hardly ever find an adult so *impolite* as to correct your pronunciation or your grammar, although occasionally he will help you with words. Mexicans are simply too courteous to take a chance on embarrassing another person.

But it's different with kids. If they trust in you, little kids will correct you if you want, or even if you don't. They can be a lot of help.

And Now, Some Fun. Most Words are the Same, but…

As you get more proficient in Spanish, you'll find that you can hardly make mistake with words that you guess. But there are exceptions. You don't want to say *marqueta* for market; it's *mercado*. *Supermarqueta* for supermarket (*supermercado*) will sound as funny to you as it does to a Mexican.

There are some misleading words. *Embarazada* in Spanish means *pregnant*, not embarrassed; here you will *have shame: tener vergüenza* (unless you are, indeed, pregnant).

I had a friend who was explaining that she was terribly hungry. She said, *tengo un hombre feroz* (ferocious)!. But she should have said *hambre* (hunger), not *hombre (*man*)*. That one syllable changed her meaning considerably.

Frankly, that was really funny, but nobody laughed!

Ordinary language is also different in ways that can surprise. Nobody objects to being called dark or light. *Güero*, roughly translated, is *Blondie*, but it's not necessarily a kind term.

A man will often call his wife *mi negra*. It's not something she would object to.

And fat or thin is not pejorative. *Hola, Gorda*, is no insult. It just means, *Hi, Fatty*. But don't try that in the US!

And since fat babies have been considered healthy, your kid may well be called your *gordo*, with no bad intentions or implications. Rather, it's intended as a complement, even though you might not believe it.

Don't Give Up

Just don't give up. Be persistent. Every little bit of Spanish you learn will come in handy. It will make life much more worthwhile in Mexico.

And I tell you, it's neat to be able to get by in *two* languages. It makes you feel good!

15

GIVE IN GRACEFULLY

Here I suggest that you just yield to an uncritical acceptance of life in the Mexican culture. You won't lose your own personal standards, but you'll be able to gain some understanding of Mexican life.

Come as a Little Child

As I see it, you have to suppress your pride and preconceptions if you want to really understand something. This means, in few words, that we have to hang loose if we want to understand anything.

And Mexico is like that. You can't go to Mexico, live there, and keep your Gringo orientation. That just doesn't work. Mexico is a gorgeous place to live, provided that you don't judge it by Gringo standards. I suppose that in some sense you could say that about France, or Germany, or China, or any place else, for that matter, but to really enjoy it you need to come to understand it, and *then* judge it by your new Mexico-Gringo personal standards.

So, *Hang loose.*

Mexico Evolved, Just as did the US

Because whatever you find, wherever you live, you must know that what you find there is what has evolved there. It's not what you think ought to have evolved there. It's what has really evolved there as the adaptation of humans to what they found there.

Same with Mexico. The Mexican culture is simply Mexican. It started with the Mexicans before Cortez arrived. It was violently changed by the Spanish with the victory of the Spanish culture of the time, with their diseases, their language, their religion, their weapons and their customs. What we see now is the result of five centuries of mellowing.

With that said, it's not yours or mine to decide if this is the way you would have liked Mexico to develop. You could ask me what I'd like to have seen, and I can tell you, but nobody is going to ask either you or me. What developed, developed. And that's it.

Living With Crowds

Unless you are used to spending a lot of time downtown in some large city, you're going to have to learn a new way of life. All of a sudden you are going to live in crowds. If you participate in Mexican life, it will be on Mexican terms, and that means…crowds and noise.

This means that you have to change your way of life. Just adapting to crowds has always been hard for me, and noise es even harder. But adapt one must.

But Take Precautions

Since not everybody is honest, that also means you have to think about what you carry with you. I haven't had my pockets picked a single time in all the time I've been in Mexico, but I have friends and relatives who have (including my elderly mother during a visit).

So don't carry your passport or other vital papers with you unless you have need. Store copies of all documents, and you might consider carrying the copies with you instead of the originals in your wallet.

Don't wear valuable jewelry, and don't carry more money than you need.

Where pickpockets are most active, such as in large markets or country fairs, the system is highly formalized so that you won't be able to escape unless you are alert. And if it happens, it isn't even easy to report it.

So take precautions, and stay alert!

Be a People-Watcher

Ladies, are you especially fond of babies? There are certainly adorable babies everywhere in this country, and almost all mothers like to have other ladies admire their children. If you visit a rural town, there will always be babies to watch.

Or do you just like to see how people are alike and different from other people? Well, just take a ride on the Mexico City Metro. You'll see a tremendous variety of people, rich and poor, dark-and light-skinned, with clothing that varies from the richest and most modern, to the very traditional, leisure clothes, and work clothes, to completely rural clothes (although there is now a scarcity of traditional country clothes on the Metro).

Or do you just like to be around kids? There are kids everywhere, adorable kids, rich kids and poor kids, clean kids and dirty, kids well dressed, and kids in rags.

I enjoy watching people. There is no better people-watching territory than Mexico!

Bring Your Kids

Speaking of little children, Mexico is changing in many ways. But one thing will never change. Mexicans love kids. In fact, kids are their chief problem. Rich and poor used to have big families, partly from religious instruction and partly just because they like them. That's why the population is so high.

16

GO AHEAD: RUIN A SERVANT!

To have a servant, or to have several servants—that is the question. It is not nobler to be self sufficient. Maybe your only way to know real Mexicans is to have servants. And, it can be dangerous to your health and purse not to have one! And let's hope your servant has real roots in the country.

Having servants is often looked down on as undemocratic or elitist in the US. Somehow, one person shouldn't have need of another person for pay to do the ordinary tasks like cooking and cleaning. One should do that oneself. That's the egalitarian democratic way.

Or so most of my US friends think. Somehow I must be pretentious, or something equally unsavory.

I really don't agree, even for the US, but I won't make a case out of it. I would personally prefer a world where there was no need for people to *be* servants. But there are plenty of people that could justify the use of servants in the US who don't have any, and there are certainly plenty of people who could use that kind of job, provided it paid barely enough. But I'm not concerned with the US here. I'm concerned with Mexico.

And I can tell you, in Mexico the servant system works. A servant doesn't make enough money, of course, but there are certain compensations that make the real wage greater than the apparent wage. It's really very important for people to be hired as servants. And it usually is not demeaning to either party, or at least, no more demeaning than having any kind of boss. It's just a way to spread employment and to make life more complete for all.

More complete?

Yes. More complete!

You see, this is just part of the overall system that eases the transition from country to city and from poverty to middle class life.

By now you understand that to my mind, the most serious problem of Mexico is its population growth. You may also understand that despite all the rhetoric, getting people out of the country and into the cities is the only real cure. In the country, kids are free. In the city, they cost. Everyone that goes to the city has fewer descendants, and normally that happens quite rapidly, in the first or second generation. And everybody that stays behind in the country will have too many descendants. An oversimplification, of course, but essentially true.

But Many Mexicans say Americans Ruin Servants

You need to understand from the start that many Mexicans, especially rich ones, claim that Americans only ruin good servants. They accustom them to higher wages, to less work, and to more time off. Frankly, I'm in favor of *ruining* them in that sense. Servants work more hours than in other jobs, and they are often treated badly. Let's have them *be worth* more and *earn* more! Still, I must admit that there are Americans that do exaggerate for a lack of experience, mostly because the idea of having servants is new to them.

And how do we do in our house? Well, our servants earn a good wage according to local standards, but not more, and they work the same hours as others. We adjust to local conditions, and we expect to do right within those limits. Probably you will, too.

My Mexican Family

My wife's family is terribly large, but I'm proud of all of them. Her parents' generation was raised in the country, and so with brothers and sisters and cousins, there was a tremendous number of them. They reproduced in the standard way, as if most kids were going to die and you needed lots of them to get a few survivors. That was true a few generations ago.

But medicine in the country was getting better and most of them survived. Since none of them owned any real estate, they all migrated out. They had to. There was no other way.

A large fraction went to the US, which was still essentially open in the old days. Almost all the rest went to Mexico City. In the case of my in-laws, my wife's mother noticed that most of the US migrants ended up as day laborers, and so she directed the family into Mexico City, where she knew there were opportunities.

She made sure that *her* kids became teachers, because that was the one profession she could understand, really the only one she could understand. She and her brothers and sisters didn't have access to more than first grade, but she had known teachers, and she knew that her kids could at least aspire to be teachers. Although there were temptations for short careers (hairdressers, mechanics, radio repairmen, and others), she wanted her kids to become something, and, without an exception, they did.

But how to survive in the big city? Well, the father of the family scrounged as best he could, and since he was a dependable worker, he finally got a permanent job.

And my mother-in-law?

She became a servant!

My wife and her brothers and sisters remember occasionally going with her as she cleaned house. Do they have bad memories of that? Not at all! There were differences, of course. But given a relatively enlightened "master-servant" tradition, there was a certain feeling of mutual respect. My mother-in-law was a good, solid worker, and she was respected for that. She had clean, disciplined kids, and so they were tolerated and even respected in an appropriate way.

That is to say, there was a complete system of values in place which involved mutual respect among people who deserved it.

As a result of the family's success in the city, my wife and her brothers and sisters became professionals. The servant system here worked to everyone's benefit. Not that servants earned decent wages. They didn't, but they did get by, and their higher goals made that possible.

Of course, there are people who don't make good bosses for anyone, and people who for reasons of personality don't make good bosses for some people. And there are lazy people, and dishonest people, and dumb people who don't make good employees, and there are good people who for some reason don't get along with some kinds of bosses. That's not new. I'm sure you've had problems with a boss that other people thought was a true gem.

It's just important to note that the boss-employee relation is one that requires work and adjustment from both sides, and even so, can't work out for everyone.

But I'm sure that you, good American that you are, will make a good and wholesome boss for someone.

So go ahead. Try.

Fringe Benefits

Of course, servant wages are meager. But there are fringe benefits, and they aren't demeaning unless you take them that way. A good servant has always been hard to find, and indeed always will be hard to find. But there's a certain self-interest in having a good and reliable servant. And a good boss, for that matter.

But beyond that, in my mother-in-law's case, her employers took an active interest in helping the family. It gave them a certain good feeling to help deserving people. And in the back of their minds, they probably recognized, as should you and I, that if you go back a few generations; our family also came out of the country. There are born hereditary aristocrats among us, but damn few. Really, we're all from out there.

So in the case of my wife's family there were fringe benefits in food, in clothes, in religious ties (godfather and godmother relation), and others. Everything helps when you are trying to get ahead.

Having Servants

Needless to say, I'm not telling you how to run the US. I do better here because I enjoy being here, and I'm no longer that competent at living in the US. When I talk about servants I do know there are problems with reasonable wages, child care, family values, drugs, theft, and others. But my gut feeling is that a decent servant system would help in the US. But that's another matter. Here I'm only talking about Mexico.

Here you *should* have servants. They will help you understand the Mexican world.

But it's also a practical matter. There are people here (like everywhere) who will rob you blind. The first line of defense is to have someone reliable around the house or apartment at all times. The easiest way is for a cleaning lady with some cooking responsibilities. But others can help too. You might have a live-in or work-in person for the garden and other masculine duties.

It all depends on your circumstances. But plan on always having someone in your place.

How to pick Servants

Networking is the current US word. You need to "network." You don't just pick up somebody off the street to work for you, nor someone who just comes up and offers herself. What you do is ask around your friends for recommendations, particularly your Mexican friends. Your friends will probably ask *their* servants, who might well have friends or relatives looking for work; it's always hard for poor people to find work, and that's not only in Mexico.

Of course, you must meet a prospective servant in the presence of people who know or recommend him or her, or who found him. This isn't a job for you by yourself, especially if you have any problems with the language. You know you'll look for signs of brightness, and especially, signs of cleanliness. You haves to set the rules and conditions, courteously, of course: live in or come in daily, infants or kids allowed or not, rules on food, etc. You'll be astounded at the number of available single mothers with tiny kids.

You also have to set the wage, and you'd better investigate local wages *before* this interview. Use a *good or very good* local wage, but not one that's double or triple the local wage, even if you think that would be more reasonable. You don't want a person that wants only to work for foreigners; you want a good, traditional Mexican. Make sure there's very formal agreement on the wage and exactly when you will pay it. You also need to be very explicit on time off, which is typically Saturday afternoon and all day Sunday. Use local terms. Later you can adjust the salary or give goods, and you can be liberal in time off. But if you don't specify normal local conditions, you are asking for trouble.

Make sure you specify a trial period. A month, then two more months is fine. You'll probably know by the time a month has gone by. If you know before a month, you can let the person go but *pay the whole month* so you won't have any moral or legal obligations.

Security and Servants

Most Mexican people are quite honest. That's a given, as much as it is in the US or Canada. But most people can be tempted, and for a poor person there are certainly many temptations around.

You need to recognize that just the presence of your things, so much better than her things, is serious. There are people who want access to your things, and they can bribe a servant. And there are people, including maids, who are just plain crooks, who only take jobs to plan how to get your things.

Here are two cases from real life. One daughter of a campesino friend of ours wanted to work and our friend asked us to take her. She didn't look promising, but to please our friend we did, giving her a place to live and some simple cleaning duties.

One day she was gone. On a hunch we checked our things. My grandmother's ring, a family heirloom, was gone.

Fortunately we were able to get it back. She had gone back home to the country. Our friend found out what had happened, and just got it back to us, with apologies.

Another case. A close friend, an MD, needed a girl to answer his office phone and run errands, mostly paying bills. Here you don't use checks to pay bills. Most are paid in cash.

He put an ad in the paper and took on a promising young woman. She seemed to be able to do everything he needed, she accepted the wage he offered, and she was obviously intelligent.

Rather too intelligent. One day she didn't show up. And when he checked, none of the bills had been paid. He also found that all her paper work: her request for employment, photo, and everything else that could identify her had also disappeared.

She had obviously taken the job just to fleece him. He was out of the money, and his records were corrupted. There was nothing he could do.

Let's look at some lessons from these cases. First, it's best if you have some kind of personal reference, so in case of problems you have some place to start looking for the person. You also do need the correct identification of a person, and you need to have a photo, and copies of all should be kept where that person has no access. The easiest way is to require a request for employment form filled out, with a photo attached. The photo can easily be one that you take, with any pretext. But if you find a person that doesn't want to be photographed, you don't want that person to have access to your things.

As everywhere, it's best not to tempt. I'm in favor of having a simple inexpensive hard-mounted wall safe that can't be carried away (you can get a tiny one for less than $100 in Mexico). Keep jewelry, money, passports and visas, and other documents in the safe. If your things are hidden in a dresser drawer beneath your underwear, for example, you can be sure that even the best of servants is going to check them out just to satisfy curiosity.

And in any case, check frequently. Don't leave money around the house. It's never a good idea, nor a nice thing, to count or flaunt money before a poor person.

So Now You Have a Servant

Now you're a master. But that doesn't mean, necessarily, *tyrant*, or *exploiter*, or despoiler of the down-trodden or less fortunate.

What it means is that now you're the boss in a boss-employee relationship, this time in which you are paying the wage!

This sets up a system of mutual responsibilities. You decide what's to be done, and you must do that in a responsible way, conscious of what you agreed to and what's reasonable, what the employee is capable of doing, in an appropriate time frame, and to a certain standard of quality. The servant is responsible for doing the contracted work, within the same constraints. You must both work within the constraints of the mutual agreement made during the interview (negotiating phase), all within the trial period.

If all goes well, if you're the appropriate boss *and* the new employee is the appropriate employee, you have just begun one of the most satisfying relationships you can have. It probably won't last forever, though it could. The prognosis of a good relation in our house has been five or ten years. Let me tell you a about a few.

Norma (that's not her real name) was from way out in the country. She had two years of schooling, but then deferred to her brother, since it was more important for men to be educated (and he went all the way open to him, which was six years of grade school in a one-room school). We found out about her from a cousin in the city.

As she grew into adolescence it became obvious that she wasn't going anywhere where she was. She lived about a half hour's walk from the nearest country road, with no electricity nor water in the house. She didn't look forward to the life she could foresee on the family property, so she escaped to the *big city* where we live, where she figured she'd have more opportunities.

She came to work with us. She did most of the cleaning and some of the cooking. She turned out to be very diligent and very trustworthy. We made sure she enrolled in school to advance as best she could, and we made time available. She did well at that, too, but she didn't choose to advance very far. After all, for her the best time for school had passed.

She became a part of the family, and we invited her to share meals with us. She accepted and ate with us, except when we had visitors. Every so often we'd drive her to the country and walk cross country to visit her family. We've even participated in family celebrations in the country, really a gorgeous experience for us.

It's hard for a girl like her to find a good husband, regardless of her talent and virtues. Most apparently available men are really out just for the conquest. She was looking for a husband, and finally fell for one, and finally became pregnant. She found out the hard way that his intentions weren't good, and ended up a single mother with a lovely baby girl. With this new change in her life she decided to leave our household after some eight years, and eventually got a better job at a school.

Now she's a frequent visitor, along with her little girl, and we keep in contact with her family, the ones that migrated to the city as well as the ones still in the country. I'm sure we have before us a lifetime relation with both. If the little girl lives up to her promise, she'll be needing help in her education. We hope she'll go all the way, to the limit of her own abilities, and we'll encourage and help her. It won't be easy for her. We'll help as we can, but it's up to her.

No let's talk about Lorena. When Norma decided to leave, she introduced us to Lorena. Lorena had finished two years of high school, and she was more comfortable with schooling in general.

She also turned out to be a good and reliable person. We helped her get into the college preparatory courses (last two years of high school), and she did well. She finally decided to go on to college. She stayed on with us for a few more years, and then figured she could make it on her own. So she left, too. But we see a lot of her, too.

You can certainly worry about protocol in relations with servants. I suppose a lot of people think there's an absolute social gap, but that's not really so. Norma and Lorena came to share our table, even as servants, once we had attained a certain intimacy. Others, including very fine, reliable people, didn't. One of the best of these, a mature matron, just didn't feel it appropriate. Of course, when we had company, even the most intimate were pure servants and did not sit with us at the table.

17

CREATIVE TOURISM I: COUNTRY BUS RIDING

One way or another, you should be a tourist, but a good, creative one. You could drive yourself out into the surrounding countryside to see what it's like, but I suggest you don't. It's not the same as taking the same bus the campesinos take to get there. Find out how to get around the small towns in your area by bus. Then do it. You'll have a better feeling for how the real Mexicans live.

To understand Mexico, you need to understand the countryside. Cities are nice and have all the amenities. But the heart of Mexico is still its countryside.

I understand people who like to live in Mexico City. There's no other place like it in the world. They say that about New York too, and in the same way. It's a place you can't exhaust. Whatever your interests, you'll find them there, and in abundance.

I also understand people who don't like to live in large cities. The biggest cities in the world also have the biggest problems in the world. I myself would like to live near enough to Mexico City to explore its depth, but far enough away to miss its police and its problems. But I can't, and probably you can't either.

But wherever you choose to live, you should be a creative tourist. Do what it takes to understand the countryside. My suggestion is that you travel like the Mexicans do, by ordinary bus.

Where to Go

If you are like me, you probably live where you have some Gringo luxury. You can take a hot shower in the morning (your water and heater mostly work), your electricity mostly works, your telephone mostly works, most of the roads in your neighborhood are paved. That is to say, you probably live in or near a city, in a zone that's hardly representative of the country. You don't live like most Mexicans, although, more and more there are plenty of Mexicans who live like you.

Just how do Mexicans live? Why don't they worry more about their water, electricity, telephones, roads, things like that? That's something you should find out. It's really a function of where they come from, and that's the country and country towns.

Squatters Heaven

First of all, if you live in a medium or large city, you can go out to the growth area around it. I love to do this. You will see some optimism and zest for life that we've lost in the US. Your understanding of population and urban dynamics from the US will fail you here, because it's simply different.

So go take a ride on a bus. Go where no Gringo has gone before.

First, just to the outskirts of the city. Look at a map. Ask your maid where the newest people in the city, the campesinos *recién llegados*, where they all live. Or if you drive in and out of the city, especially a place like Mexico City, you might see the outskirts of the city under construction. Often the highway areas are more mature, and the new communities are in areas not so easily reached.

Once you know where they are, just take a bus ride. Leave early. Your maid can tell you how to go. You can be sure there are buses, because buses go everywhere! Just take the bus as far as it goes, and get off.

Remember where you were, and how to get back. (You can get a clue by reading the return sign from inside the bus.) As you walk around you will see a scramble of cardboard or tarpaper shacks, temporary structures of all kinds, and depending on its age, some solid concrete block houses.

You will also see hordes of kids, streets that are improvised, and the infrastructure will vary according to the city's foresight. Typically you will see electric lines scattered around, available legally or illegally to almost everybody. But you'll see hydrants widely scattered and people toting buckets of water to their houses.

You can read about people squatting on the land, or "buying" it from somebody who may or may not have a valid deed. But all the people that have built their own houses will eventually get title to them. It's not like the US where you simply have no rights if you're a really poor person.

There's a spirit of optimism, rather a frontier life, for people who live in these neighborhoods. They are building something with their own hands, and it will be legally theirs some day. Are the kids dirty? They are, but that's part of the equation. Do they have problem with infrastructure? They do, but that doesn't matter. They always have bus service to the rest of the city, where they can work, and here they can live. Sooner or later the city will build schools here, and a church has probably already been started. Their kids are getting schooling either here or in the next community. Today's tarpaper walls will be concrete block some time soon. Life is getting better!

Out to Rural Communities

When I first visited the outskirts of cities, I was depressed. I didn't have anybody to explain it to me like I'm doing for you. I thought of the rich exploiting the poor, revolutionary solutions and the like. You might have the same reaction.

But that wasn't the picture, as I came to understand. There is such a thing as grinding poverty, but that is fairly rare in the outskirts of Mexican cities. These are the way stations on the trip from the country to the city. In a few years, the area will be built with solid houses, infrastructure will be in place. In addition to elementary schools you'll have high schools if the school-age population is big enough.

But how can these people stand to live under these conditions? You need to go deeper into Mexican society to understand. And that means, go to the small towns in the country where many of these people come from.

These are quiet towns. They have their own rhythms of life, and they are worth seeing. So plan your trip again, again with the help of your maid if you can. I can't really tell you much more than to reassure you that wherever you go by bus, you can come back the same way. Look at a map, perhaps, for the end-of-the-line towns, or the towns on the lowest category of roads. Then ask around to find out how to get there.

As I said, go, preferably in the morning. The far-out towns in my area are about two hours away. I get dressed a bit warm (the towns in my area are in the mountains), and I wait on the street, a bit earlier than scheduled, since the third-class buses can come earlier or later by, say, a half hour. And then we go.

The trip goes through countryside I don't otherwise see, onto unpaved roads, where I'd be afraid to drive. But the scenery is fascinating, In my area I even see tree ferns, something I wouldn't otherwise see. Finally we get there.

The driver and his assistant are certainly going back. For them there's nothing here. Not even a place to sit and eat. So they sit or sleep in the bus until it's time to leave.

But you can prowl the town. Walk the length and breadth. Stop in the little shops and ask what things are, where roads go…You'll be amazed at the calm…hardly any cars, probably people moving about on horses and donkeys, children everywhere…If you're lucky, somebody will want to talk more, and invite you in for coffee, or a beer, or a snack.

There's really not much you can do in these towns. That's part of what you are going to understand. You see why people don't go back regularly once they leave. Mostly they go back to see their parents or for the fiesta of the community saint.

Out to the Countryside

But towns don't show you the true isolation of the countryside. To understand that you'll need to go even farther, and for that you'll need the help of someone with family way out in the country. Your servant, maybe, or a friend of hers.

You should make the effort. This is the way you really get some perspective on the real Mexico and real Mexicans. Mexico is becoming an urban country, just like the US, but that's a long way off. Real Mexico, today, still has its roots in the country, and the majority of Mexicans are still familiar with their roots.

How to do this? It probably won't be easy. Somehow you need to get somebody to take you. You just don't appear in a rancho unannounced without a person known to the locals.

For most of us, it takes an invitation by a person who's fairly recently migrated to the city. These workers are mostly in construction and manual trades, security guards and night watchmen, and in house servants. For most of us, the easiest persons are the house servants because they know us and we know them, and there is mutual trust.

You need an invitation, of course. The most normal is to celebrate a local saint's day, or birthday of someone, wedding, baptism of a child, something that is honestly celebrated. You'll want to go with the person you know, of course.

It is never an obligation in the eyes of your host to take gifts. It is always preferable in every way, but you must be discreet. Remember that these people will never show that they have a need, but probably they are living at a subsistence level, eating what they grow locally. They really don't have much for outsiders, though they will always share what little they have.

This is a case where using a car is often preferable, simply because the really rural zones are not well served by buses, and in any case, everybody, probably including you, will be taking packages. There are things that subsistence farmers can't easily prepare, and those are things you should take. The most obvious is cooking oil, easily bought at stores in the city.

I'm not going to tell you much about these visits because they are all different. They depend on the part of the country, the type of farming, local resources, whether there are schools in the area, and many other things. Still, in general, you should go early enough so you can spend hours there, and still leave while there's light, so you can find your way home.

Remember that these proto-Mexicans are extremely courteous, very religious, and exceedingly polite. You'll probably find they are among the most admirable people in your life. You'll probably want to be invited back. If all goes well, you will be.

18

CREATIVE TOURISM II:
THE JOYS OF MARKETS

Shopping in markets is fun. It's the Mexican reflex way of buying food, clothes, even cars, almost everything an ordinary person needs. You need to visit all the markets you can, just to see how they work. I like to visit early, as they are setting up, and during the day as they are operating. Even malls have days when they operate like markets.

It's something of an adventure to travel as I suggest, but exploring markets is easy. You just go. In Mexico, almost anything an ordinary person wants to buy for personal use he can buy in one or another market. Real estate is the only exception that comes to mind.

Historic Markets

When Hernán Cortez arrived at Tenochtitlán, he found one of the largest cities of those times. That has become Mexico City, for a while the largest city of these times, now with some 20,000,000 inhabitants.

He was also astounded to find a fully organized market system, offering a wide variety of products, including much more than food. It is a tradition that survives even today in almost all parts of Latin America. We have historical descriptions of the Tlatelolco market in Tenochtitlán and a large, beautifully prepared model in the Museum of Anthropology in Mexico City. The similarity to today's markets is evident.

Central Markets

You want to see where your food comes from? Visit the food market downtown. There are some exceptions, now, but most cities and town have major markets in the center of the city as well as neighborhood markets. Wherever you are, you should visit these markets. They are important for understanding Mexico. And it's fun!

The food markets are always organized if they are large enough. The meat and poultry are in one part, fish in another, vegetables in another, and fruit in another, though sometime fruit and vegetables are mixed. In Mexico City, the markets, themselves, are specialized, with, say, fruit and vegetables in one, meat in others, and so on. There's even a Metro stop dedicated to a market, the gigantic Merced market, with mostly fruit and vegetables.

But there are also markets of anything else you might want to buy. Let me make a short list of specialized Mexico City markets in addition to permanent food markets. There are quite a few of almost all of these.

Markets on wheels (once or twice a week in designated areas, with food and other goods)

　　Flowers
　　Clothing
　　Hardware, including specialized
　　Electrical goods
　　Locks and keys
　　Repair parts for gas stoves and other systems
　　Construction materials
　　Household goods

Animals in general, and pets
Plants
Handicrafts
Used goods
Black market goods
Cars

and there are certainly many others.

But Why Even Mention Markets?

Why should I mention markets in the first place?

It's just that the dependence on markets is another way that Mexicans are different from Americans. The reflex of a Mexican is not to go looking for things at the mall or the supermarket. It's to go look in the market. There are even people who as a diversion explore the markets, just like Americans who explore malls just to see what's there.

I must admit that more and more teenagers are learning to hang out in malls, just as in the US and Canada. But the adults are still oriented towards markets.

Creative Market Gazing

I find great pleasure going to markets, and almost everybody that comes to visit does, too. The smaller the town (providing it's large enough to have a permanent market), the more interesting the market.

A market has what people buy and use. If you see an odd fruit, or device, or item of clothing, it's worth identifying, because it's something that's used.

First I suggest you check out the fruits and vegetables. You are bound to find fruit that you can't identify, and they are worth trying. And you can see what a housewife feels she needs to cook with, or to clean with. It's all there. These are not the imported goods from the supermarket. These are what ordinary women need and use.

The same with hardware. If you're on the Yucatán peninsula, you'll see specialized anchors and hooks for hanging hammocks, and of course, you'll find hammocks. If you're in the northern part of Mexico you'll find other things, like cowboy boots and leather belts. I'm sure you'll even find things even you want to take home with you. Some are kitchen goods you remember from your grandmother but that you can no longer find in stores in the US.

For example, even though I don't live in the southern part of Mexico, now I have hammock anchors in my walls and hammocks to mount in them, something that always intrigues visitors from the US!

19

AND NOW, WELCOME TO MEXICO!

Finally and most important, you want to know if you are really welcome in Mexico? Well, let me set your mind at ease. This is one place in the world where you are welcome. I'll tell you some of the many different ways you can come and something of what you can expect. But the one thing that's most important for you to know is that Mexicans are, above all, a hospitable people. They love having guests. Don't stay away because you think you're not wanted here.

I told you that my chapter on the police was the hardest to write. That will probably be the one that makes the most people angry with me.

Well, this is certainly the easiest to write. Everyone wants you to come. People will probably get mad at me for other things I say, but nobody will get mad at me for showing you how to come and get to understand Mexico.

You've heard me talk a little of xenophobia in Mexico, and I've shown you some major differences in the way Mexicans think and live. Does that mean they don't want to see you in their country?

I hope you didn't get that idea because it's not true. Mexicans welcome visitors much more than other people, certainly more than the Americans. And it's not just that they want tourist money. In fact, most people don't even think about such things. They just like having visitors.

How to Come

There are certainly many ways you might come here. Now I'm going to play *travel advisor*, or at least travel *promoter*. I'm going to spell out, in a very simple way, some of your options for coming here, and just what each way will get you. Frankly, you need a reason to come. And there are certainly many reasons, as you'll see.

You can come here for a short stay without a visa, just by walking across the border from the US, though it's always better to have a passport. You can come to major tourist resorts, and you won't even need any knowledge of Spanish to survive. You can come to non-touristy places, and just relax or explore if you wish. You can retire and live here. You can come here as an employee of a business, or to start a business. You're welcome in every one of these ways, and many others, too.

Just Walk Across

If you happen to be anywhere near the border, you just need to cross over the border. You need to carry some identification, and then, you just walk across, normally by crossing a bridge. You can stay for a day at a time without any problem, even without having a passport and visa.

Mexican cities on the US border have different rules than the rest. They are really binational cities since their economic life depends on people on both sides of the border. As an example, Laredo in the US and Nuevo Laredo in Mexico are a single concentration of people, and it is just an accident of politics that the two are in different countries.

So, Mexican border cities allow the temporary crossing of American or Canadian tourists without more than, say, a driver's license as identification. Still, I always recommend you have a passport with you in this situation. Passports are not expensive, and they are the most trusted of identification documents.

I won't say that border towns are the best introduction to Mexico or Mexican life. They are certainly the easiest and cheapest, but they are severely distorted just because they *are* border cities. They mostly sell only touristy things, and a good part of their inhabitants are oriented towards things tourists want. The worst parts are the *Boys' Towns* that several have, but still, all of them have stores and restaurants with incredible food, and they certainly are a genuine part of Mexico.

What will you see? Towns that live off their position on the border, towns that live off of tourist money, Mexicans in the tourist business. Even Mexicans with permission to work on the American side. It's Mexico, but just a small part of it.

Take a Package Tour

Every tourist agency in the US has package tours for you alone or for groups. These are the next easiest way to come.

You can come and see just as much (or just as little) of Mexico as you want, and you will know just what it costs in advance. If you have no knowledge of Mexico and you just want to start, this is not a bad way. You'll get your documents in order (a passport, of course) and you'll see how easy it is to get a tourist visa. You'll see how to convert dollars to pesos (and *vice versa)* and handle pesos. You'll settle into your hotel, and you'll see how many other hotels there are. You'll be able to go out into restaurants and stores not included in your package. And it is Mexico, but seen the easiest way.

Typically you buy the package, get on a plane, (with your group if it's a group package), and everything is arranged for you. This is an easy, exciting and interesting way to take time from your job. It's ideal for the first time out.

You can go to Cancún, stay at a luxurious hotel, and see what the gorgeous turquoise Carribean and the Mayan ruins look like.

Or you might go to Acapulco, or Zihuatanejo, or Acapulco, or Mazatlán, sample these gorgeous Pacific Ocean beaches, and sample their night life.

There are package tours to many parts of Mexico, and they all serve as an easy introduction to the country.

And nothing keeps you in line on these tours. You go out on to the town, scour the shops, sample the restaurants, start to practice your Spanish, and all with your living arranged for you so you don't have to worry about anything.

Just Fly In and Tour

You want to see Mexico City, or Guadalajara, or Monterrey, or wherever? Well, you can just go! It's best to make a hotel reservation in advance, but even that normally isn't necessary. Since most Mexican cities have an excess of hotel rooms available, if all else fails, you can just come and find a room when you arrive. (However, don't try that on special holidays like Christmas and New Year or Easter if you're going to the touristy areas like Acapulco, because there will be Mexican tourists as well as foreign tourists all competing for accommodations.)

This is the first option where you are on your own. You make your plans and arrange your flight. You reserve a hotel room (or your travel agent does it for you if you wish). You fly in, and pass through Immigration. You get your baggage and you pass through Customs. You get a taxi and go to your hotel. And you will have done it all yourself.

Then you are on your own. You might want to take some packaged bus tours, or you can just go where you want and see what you want to see.

You'll certainly be interacting with more Mexicans this way. You'll need to practice a bit of your Spanish. And you'll learn more about how Mexicans live and do things.

If You Have a Mexican Friend

If you have the good luck to have a Mexican or other friend living in Mexico, that's even better. Hotel life has its advantages, but there's nothing like getting closer to real Mexican life.

You just do the same as above, and go to your friend's house. And if you've been reading this book, you'll start getting into the real Mexican life.

If You're a Business Man

Check at your nearest Mexican consulate first. In the past, a tourist visa was often enough for most visits, but the requirements could change.

Here you just come to a hotel, and visit your clients. There's nothing to it. And it gets easier each time.

You Come to Live as Employee of a Company

Suppose you are an employee of a Mexican company, or an American company, or some combination of both. This is going to be more complicated (but not very complicated) and more expensive. It's imperative that you consult a consulate for the requirements, that is, unless your company takes care of the red tape.

You come the same way, but now you come to live. Now I think this book will really be useful to you.

You Come to Live for Any Reason

People tend to fall in love with Mexico. (Take me, for instance!) If you have the money, or if you can earn money some way while you're here, you can just choose to live here.

If you want to retire here, there are special rules. You need to see your nearest Mexican Consul to find out just what the rules are. In essence, you have to have more income than US Social Security gives you, but given sufficient income, there are many fine alternatives.

The American Embassy in Mexico City

I certainly haven't covered many of the problems you may have in Mexico City, either as a visitor or as a long time resident. For that we have the excellent American Embassy, in downtown Mexico City, on the gorgeous, impressive avenue called Paseo de la Reforma.

The embassy has a World Wide Web site at http://www.usembassy.org.mx, which gives you the option of an English and Spanish version. The English language at http://www.usembassy.org.mx/emenu.html gives you access to various subjects, which at this writing are:

Services for American Citizens

Services for Mexicans

Directory of the Embassy and Consulates in Mexico

General Information About the United States

Priority Issues for the U.S. Embassy

Benjamin Franklin Library in Mexico City

Press and Media

The office of most use to you by mail will be:

Citizen Services Office Room 101

Paseo de la Reforma 305

Col. Cuauhtemoc

Telephone: 5211-0042

They have handouts on Living in Mexico, Retirement in Mexico, Your Health in Mexico, lists of medical doctors and hospitals, and other things. They are universally polite and helpful for American citizens. However the crush of applications for tourist visas is so great that there is a severe loss of courtesy in the employees of that section, something that is deeply resented by Mexicans of all classes.

My final message is: You're welcome in Mexico. Feel free to come and visit. You'll have a good time.

-The End-

A Final Note

The author invites readers to visit his site on the World Wide Web, **www.Hello_Mexico.com**. He intends to post some of their comments, both good and bad, for general discussion. Of course, correspondence can be either in English or in Spanish.

It's important that Mexicans have access to this book. A Spanish version will soon be published by iUniverse.com under the title, *Hola México*. Since the translation was made by the author, it should accurately reflect its content and concepts, even if it lacks the beauty of fine prose in Spanish. Hopefully, Mexicans will recognize that the book is an affectionate introduction to their country, not at all a criticism.

Both versions will be available online in iUniverse.com's Free Reader's Library at **http://www.iuniverse.com/library/**. They are certainly much easier to read on paper than on a computer screen, but this unique service makes them completely available to everybody with access to the Internet.

Printed in the United States
33832LVS00006B/146